Tempus ORAL HISTORY *Series*

Colchester
voices

BOROUGH OF COLCHESTER

POLICE NOTICE

EVACUATION

TO THE INHABITANTS OF

.... {Road
{Street
{Avenue

The Government has decided that Evacuation from the Town must take place at once.

You must therefore assemble at...

by.......................... a.m. on the ....
                          p.m.

to go to... Station.

YOUR TRAIN is due to leave the above Station

at.................... a.m. on the ....
                   p.m.

Your train will be numbered...

By Order

H. C. STOCKWELL, Lt.-Col.,

Chief Constable.

Printed by E. N. MASON & SONS, LTD., Arclight Works, Colchester

A notice of evacuation from the Second World War.

Tempus ORAL HISTORY *Series*

Colchester
voices

Compiled by
Patrick Denney

TEMPUS

First published 2000
Copyright © Patrick Denney, 2000

Tempus Publishing Limited
The Mill, Brimscombe Port,
Stroud, Gloucestershire, GL5 2QG

ISBN 0 7524 1884 X

Typesetting and origination by
Tempus Publishing Limited
Printed in Great Britain by
Midway Clark Printing, Wiltshire

To Anne, Linda and Alistair

A group photograph showing some of the people interviewed by the Colchester Recalled Oral History Group, many of whom are featured in this publication.

Contents

Acknowledgements

It goes without saying that I am greatly indebted to all those persons whose stories and experiences appear throughout the pages of this book. They have willingly shared their innermost thoughts and experiences and without their help the following work would not have been possible.

I would like to thank further the following respondents and the relatives and friends of others who have kindly made available treasured family photographs to illustrate the text and for allowing, where applicable, the memories of their deceased loved ones to be published: Doug Appleby, Ethel Appleby, Jack and Betty Austin, Tom Bateman, Derek Blowers, Mrs I. Bones, Maureen Cardy, Evina Cooper, Albert and Agnes Cork, Paul Gallifant, Bob Gentry, Marcel Glover, Keith Gunton, John Hedges, Nina Markham, Edna Mills, Roy and Linda Munson, Daphne Pushman, Janet and Michael Read, Joan Reynolds, Elsie Seabourne, Reg Shelley, Chris Smith, Bill Warner and Arthur Went.

I would also like to thank Pauline Day for her work in transcribing many of the interviews and my son, Stephen Denney, for help in producing some of the computerized illustrations.

Finally, I must thank fellow historian Andrew Phillips who was responsible for nurturing my initial interest in oral history back in the late 1980s and for his continued encouragement and support through the years.

The fish pond in the Castle Park, which was created in the shape of a Roman bath, 1920s.

Introduction

The following collection of reminiscences was originally compiled as part of an oral history project undertaken in conjunction with the Colchester Recalled Oral History Group between 1989 and 1999. More than 500 interviews were completed by the group, resulting in some 2,000 hours of unique and historically valuable recordings, mostly in the form of in-depth life-story discussions tracking the experiences of those interviewed from their earliest memories to the present day. In the main, the recordings relate to how life was lived in the Colchester area during the period 1900-1950, although a few of the older respondents could go back a little further. The experiences and memories contained in this collection were extracted from sixty-three interviews completed by the author during the course of the project (which, incidentally, is still progressing), and are fully representative of the group's findings as a whole. It has certainly been a pleasure and, indeed, a privilege to have shared in the exercise; the time spent visiting people in the privacy of their homes, listening as they have shared and recounted their memories, has been among the most rewarding of my life.

The oldest person interviewed was born in 1884 and as a teenager attended Queen Victoria's funeral at Windsor in 1901. At the time of the interview she was approaching 107 and was still able to read without the use of spectacles. Most of the respondents, however, were somewhat younger, having been born during the period 1900-1910. As such, they have lived to experience most of the major events and changes of the twentieth century, including two world wars and man's historic landing on the moon. The next largest group interviewed were born between 1911 and 1920, and the youngest participant, a relative youngster, was born in 1934. Many can recall the days of horse-drawn carriages and trams, of music halls and variety theatres, of periods of hardship and depression and, for some, the horrifying experience of trench warfare in the fields of Flanders. Almost without exception, despite many having received a poor upbringing by modern standards, they speak of the past with affection and recount happy memories with no regrets of their lot in life; after all, most people were in the same boat. Few homes of the early period could boast the luxury of an inside lavatory or bathroom, and family life was certainly what you made it; there was no television or radio to keep one company and for many families a get-together and sing song around the piano on a Friday or Saturday night would have been the highlight of the week.

The recordings have provided a unique insight into how life was lived during an age which is fast becoming forgotten as we move into the twenty-first century. And in the same way that we would value being able to listen to a first-hand account from the life of one of our own ancestors from earlier times, the present collection of memories and experiences will prove to be of immense value to future generations as they seek to make sense of life in the twentieth century.

Although the book is aimed primarily at the general readership and does not attempt to analyse or comment on any of the opinions expressed, it is perhaps fitting that a few words should be mentioned regarding the nature and value of oral evidence as a primary source for constructing local and family histories. The very fact that oral evidence is produced in a retrospective situation where respondents are often recalling to mind events from the distant past, and are therefore detached by time from the subject matter, goes against the prevailing principle of many mainstream historians who uphold the belief that contemporariness should be the prime requirement of any historical source. They would argue that the practice seeks to collect evidence which was not produced at the time and which invariably will reflect present interests. The evidence is also being collected in a changed culture and is therefore not vulnerable to the pressures and biases of the period which produced it, although it would, of course, be shaped by the biases of its own day. Another area which gives rise to some concern is the ability of an elderly informant to recall accurately events from the past. It is, of course, accepted that a person's ability to remember events from the past does tend to deteriorate with advancing years, but studies among the elderly have shown that under normal circumstances, and providing that the person is enjoying normal health, the problem of memory and recall should be no more serious than that of a younger person, particularly with regard to their long-term recall. During the course of the present interviews this premise was tested on numerous occasions with positive results. It is also apparent that the memory process depends not only upon individual comprehension, but also upon the informant having an interest in the subject matter being discussed.

On a final note, regardless of what arguments or criticisms may be brought to bear upon the subject, the collecting of oral evidence will remain a valuable and, in many ways, unique historical source providing us with a more personalized and perhaps truer picture of the past which is often lacking in the official record. Of course, where applicable, one would seek to corroborate the oral data with that from documentary sources, but where this is not possible then we must surely accept the spoken word for what it is and allow its value be established from within its own trustworthiness and authenticity.

A 1940s advertisement for Hugh Markham's pawnbroking business. Note the firm's official slogan: 'To borrow or spend, Markham's your friend'. (See also p. 62)

CHAPTER 1
Home and Family

Jack Ashton aged ninety.

Sixpence on the Rent

Good gracious alive! There was no thought of flush toilets until the compulsory came in, then the landlords had to lay it. And all it meant for my mother's landlord – all he had to do was to put a bit of lead pipe through, and at that time that would have cost no more than a pound, and he put sixpence on the rent. Forever, that was – that was a rise in the rent of sixpence. No, I don't think any working-class people had a bathroom until the council started building houses. People had got so used to bringing the bath in, having it in the scullery or perhaps in front of the fire to have their bath. It was nothing unusual to see a bath hanging out – outside the back door on the wall of the terraced houses.

Jack Ashton (born 1902)

Seen and Not Heard

I was born in 1892 and I've lived in this same house since 1900. I remember my parents as being fairly strict – they kept us in order. We had to clean our shoes at a certain time, eat at a certain time and go to bed at a certain time. And at mealtimes we were not allowed to speak unless we were spoken to, that was the rule: children were to be seen and not heard. We were brought up to respect authority; if you went out and saw somebody that you knew, you had to raise your hat, especially if it was the parson – if you met him you had to nearly bow down to the ground. Of course, at that time of day everybody went to church – if you didn't go to church you wasn't recognized. Whenever you went to get a job you had to have a reference from the parson and if you couldn't get one you never got a job.

Sidney Murrells (born 1892)

Scrub Night

The house had nothing much inside and I would say that we were quite poor when we moved to Colchester. There was a gas light bracket on the wall and after a few weeks mother bought a mantle and then later a globe because the wind kept blowing the mantle to pieces. We had three bedrooms, two living rooms and a kitchen downstairs. No bathroom – you had to bathe in the kitchen in a galvanized bath. Friday night was 'scrub night' for all of us when we were younger, but when I got older mother would have the bath ready for me when I got home about ten o'clock. There was a coal house outside and a toilet and just a tap at the sink. There was no hot water and the cooking was done on a range, an open grate with an oven which was heated from the fire – even in the summer! Wash day was always on a Monday, with the old bath in the sink. People didn't seem to wear so many clothes

at that time. Us kids had a shirt, a jersey and trousers but no underclothes.

Bob Allen (born 1906)

No Bathroom

I was born in a small house in Greenstead Road. It had two bedrooms, a sitting room and a kitchen. Mother and father slept in one of the bedrooms and the rest of us eight children slept in the other and on put-you-ups in the room downstairs. There was no bathroom and if we wanted to have a bath we used to have to go to town. We also had a tin bath outside and sometimes in the summer some of us would get out in the shed and have a bath, especially father when he came home from the foundry. We got the water from a tap outside, heated it in the copper and then carried it out in buckets.

Charles Herbert (born 1897)

Three to a Bed

I was born at Playford in Suffolk in 1901 and was brought to Great Bromley when I was about three months old. We lived at The White House which had three bedrooms and two main rooms downstairs. There was no bathroom, but not much fuss was made about bathing in those days. Mother had a big old zinc bath which was also used for washing. Saturday night was bath night and if there was room two would go in together. The bath would be put in front of the fire and it was an exciting time. You hear so much about sex today but to us it didn't mean anything – we knew that we were made differently but it didn't create any curiosity. And we all slept in

Marcel and Jane Glover enjoy a bath by the fire in the 1950s.

the same bed – three to a bed. I never knew my father's family, but I can remember my grandmother on my mother's side. She was a tall, stately lady and everyone was in fear and trembling of her. She was so precise, a very dignified lady and she never seemed to have a hair out of place. She always had a white ruffle round her neck and very often a cap on her head. She also often used to wear black – always a dark dress – and great voluptuous aprons with a huge bow at the back. She was widowed quite young and used to take in washing to help make ends meet. She would be working nearly every day and would hang the washing out to dry on a big fence in the back garden.

Ethel Appleby (born 1901)

Kind but Firm

I was born at Crockleford in 1903 and was one of thirteen children – six girls and seven boys. We were all born at home – no maternity homes in those days. The nurse used to come from Ardleigh and the doctor from Manningtree. Our first home had just two bedrooms, a living room, kitchen and a wash house. Mum and Dad slept in one room and the children in the other, some at the head of the bed and some at the foot. We probably slept four or five in a bed – I can remember my mother saying that she had ten children not earning a penny. My father used to work at the gasworks and got paid about a pound a week – he thought that was a wonderful wage. He used to walk to work

Drawing water from a well, c. 1910.

across the fields from Crockleford to the Hythe and then work an eight-hour shift as a stoker – which was very hard manual work – before walking home. I can remember my parents as being kind but firm – they had to be with us lot – and father's word was his bond. If he promised you something nice you got it, and if he promised you a hiding you got it. That's what they are missing today. If we did something wrong we would get a smack on the behind with the hand. Mother used to say 'that's the best place to hit them, you can't break any bones there.'

Arthur Went (born 1903)

No Fertilizers

When father had finished work on the farm he would come home and work in the garden – no going out like they do today. Looking back, you can't compare the vegetables today with what we had in the garden. Everything was natural, no fertilizers, and they used to put chalk and lime on the garden. They also used to use horse manure or cow dung, but I think it was the sewage from the toilets that kept the ground going.

Ethel Appleby (born 1901)

Water from the Well

We used to have to get our water from the well. There were eight houses that all used that one well and they used to come with baths and buckets and deeve it out with a crome – that's a long pole with a snap thing on the end – and you put the handle of the pail in the snap and then dropped the pail in the well and teaved it down and brought the water up. The toilet was down the bottom of the garden. A good many had buckets and a good many had what they call privies, which is a big hole, bricked round and emptied about once a year, onto the garden.

Arthur Went (born 1903)

Never without Water

Our well used to be just in front of the back door. We used to pull it up with a crome, I've pulled hundreds of buckets up in my time. And that's how we got the water and the well never ran dry. It got ever so low at times and Dad used to say to Mum, 'Be careful with the water dear, we're getting down', but we were never without water.

I've got tons now but I don't waste it. I just feel, 'Oh, I mustn't waste that'. I think I'm still at Crockleford, I suppose, I don't put into my bowl no more than I want. I don't think we should waste water.

Hilda Went (born 1907)

Emptied Once a Week

Every house in Rowhedge had what most people called a 'thunder box'. It was just a hut at the bottom of the garden, probably about three feet square and six feet high. It had a small hatch in the back of it, a seat in it and under the seat was a fairly large bucket. There was a system by which the farmer here, Mr Robinson, used to get two of his men, Mr Beales and Mr Richardson, to bring a cart round with a big open-topped

Remains of an outside privy at Wivenhoe, Essex.

hopper. They covered the whole village in a week so that each household had their bucket emptied once a week. And what they did was to leave the cart somewhere adjacent to where you lived, then they would come up your garden path and go to the thunder box, open the hatch, get the bucket out, take it back to the hopper, empty it in, bring the bucket back and off they would go to the next place and so on round the whole village. If you encountered that when you were out at night you ran quickly because you could smell it coming. Then of course at the end of the night they took it up the hill, just above Rowhedge, and deposited it on the field.

Albert Cork (born 1911)

The interior of a three-hole privy.

A Proper Little Building

The toilet was in the garden and Dad used to have to empty it. It was a proper little building with tiles on the roof like your house and a nice door with a latch, and I think it was a cement floor, I'm sure it was. And nice wooden seats – Mum used to keep the tops scrubbed every time. They were lovely and clean and a rug on the floor, or mat, to put your feet on so it wasn't so cold. And there was a high seat for us bigger ones and Mum and Dad, and then there was a little short seat for the little children with a little bucket underneath, like a little pot.

Hilda Went (born 1907)

Lucky Crick

I was born in 1906 and was the youngest of seven boys. My father, Alfred Crick, was born in Knaresborough, Yorkshire, but when he came this way I don't know. He worked at the Old Heath brickfields along with my grandfather and several of my brothers. I can just remember my grandfather, Zachariah, who had served in the Grenadier Guards during the Crimea. He was about eighty when he died and, being a veteran of the Crimea, was given a real military funeral. They couldn't get the Grenadiers to attend so they asked for the Gordon Highlanders, who were stationed in Colchester, to come along instead. I didn't go to the funeral but I saw the procession go past the house from our gateway. I remember being told that when my grandfather was a young lad, before he joined the Army, he had worked on a barge called the *Bramble* which used to travel out of Mistley up to the north of England to take on coal. Well apparently on one of these trips they ran into a terrible storm which lasted for several days. When he finally arrived home, wet through to the skin, he fell down on the hearth rug and slept for two days. He refused to go to sea again in the *Bramble* and the captain took on another two hands. On the *Bramble*'s next voyage it ran into another storm, broke its bottom and went down and the two new hands were drowned. After that Zachariah was always known as 'Lucky Crick' in the Mistley area.

Les Crick (born 1906)

Five Bob a Week Rent

I was born in Canterbury Road in 1901. My mother and father had moved into the house when it was new. We had three bedrooms, a nice stairway, a front room, a living room, a kitchen and an outside toilet. They paid five bob a week rent for that. After my father died when I was about nine, my mother used to have to take in washing and us kids used to have to go and get it from up Creffield Road way. Me and my young sister Con used to have to walk all the way carrying this basket full of washing through the Barracks and across the Abbey Fields. We had gas lighting downstairs and used candles to go to bed. I remember once when mum did some washing for the people who kept the shop at the bottom of Canterbury Road, and to her annoyance the man had brought the empty basket back on a Sunday morning. Well I saw mum come through the front room, I expect she'd got her madness up, and she threw the basket across the table and it hit this hanging gas mantle which went all over the show. Oh dear, I can see that now: we were just having

Zachariah Crick, Crimean war veteran, 1830-1910.

our breakfast and this mantle was coming down all over the place. After that she had it moved onto the side wall.

Margaret Golby (born 1901)

Wages Were So Low

Many people used to use oil and gas lamps for lighting their houses. The paraffin business was good in those days. You'd either have an oil lamp on the table or perhaps a little gas bracket fitted over the chimney breast. That was a bare flare until the incandescent mantle came into being.

We had oil lamps – one for the front room, where you only went in on a Sunday, and one in the living room. If we had a fire in the front room on a Sunday that was a special occasion because fuel was about 1s or 1s 6d a hundredweight which was quite expensive inasmuch as wages were so low – my father never got no more than 30s a week. In the living room we had an open grate, with an oven alongside where mother would do the cooking and there'd be a kettle on top. Mother had to cook how the money went. I could tell you what we were going to have for dinner from day to day because there was no change, no variety, the money wouldn't allow it. Sunday would always be meat and vegetables and cold meat on Monday. There used to be a little pie shop in Butt Road called McCluskeys – everybody knew it – and I used to take a pudding basin round there with a tanner and get a bit of Yorkshire pudding, some gravy, some vegetables and a bit of meat and my mother used to eke that out for our dinner.

Jack Ashton (born 1902)

Tea on the Rec

I was born in Victor Road in 1903 and lived there until I got married. The house had a little lobby, a front room, a living room, kitchen and three bedrooms upstairs. You had to be in bed at a certain time, if they could catch you. In the wintertime you sat there, you had to make your own amusement, and we would play until about eight but in the summertime we'd be on the Recreation Ground until past nine o'clock. There were swings and all that up there. We'd come home from school and say, 'Can we take tea on the Rec, Mum?' and she would say we could. We would have bread and butter and sugar and a bottle of water. We'd go up there and have our tea and then either our brother or sister would come and try and find us, but we would hide in the hedge. When we got home we would get, 'Where've you been?' 'On the Rec, Mum.' At first we used to have an oil lamp and candles upstairs and if you'd got a candle alight in the bedroom Dad would know it and he'd be on tenterhooks until you blew it out. We would lie there reading, tight to the candle to see it. Then the gas came which was a jet, on the wall, with mantles. We had them downstairs in the front room, but no gas upstairs. We had to take a candle or oil lamp up, but more often than not you got into bed in the dark.

Joe Lawrence (born 1903)

A Character

There used to be a chimney sweep who lived opposite who would charge about threepence to sweep your chimney, but my mother used to do her own to save money. She would wait until she had a fire going in the grate and then light a lump of newspaper and put it up the chimney. And there would be soot coming down and smoke going out the top and she's say 'I hope old Ramplin [the sweep] is looking'. It used to tickle her pink to think that he could look and see what see was doing. Oh, she was a character was my mother, she really was.

Margaret Golby (born 1901)

Killing the Pig

About once a year father would buy a pig from the market or a farmer, a suckling pig, very cheap. Mother would feed it up and bring it up to about ten score [pounds] and round about autumn time, a butcher, a man named Rogers, who lived down Hythe Hill, would come and kill the pig for you. They would have a round stool to lay the pig on, put a noose round its nose, and then the butcher would do his stuff. He'd cut the pig's throat and bleed it and after that it would be hoisted up and hung on its hind legs. I remember Mother had a busy time getting ready for that. They had to have a large tub, about four foot across, for the pig to be scolded in, and the water had to got ready for that. The pig would then be dipped into the tub and its hairs all scraped off so it was nice and clean. It would then be left for a day before the butcher would come back and carve it all up. It would be cut through the middle, all the insides taken out and the 'pluck' would be reserved for the butcher – he would often take that for killing the pig. Some of the local lads would come round to see the pig killed because there was an end result – when the bladder was removed they were all chasing for it so they could blow it up and play football with it. That was the only way they could get a football in those days.

Les Crick (born 1906)

Nobody Starved

I was born in Greenstead Road in 1907. There were no maternity homes in them days; you had a woman come from the

Les Crick and his mother, Jane, in 1907.

parish. I had five brothers and three sisters – I was the youngest. My two eldest brothers, George and Dick, went to school at the vicarage and mother paid threepence a week for the parson to teach them. All the others went to a school in Greenstead. My aunties and sister used to work for Mrs Gooch at Wivenhoe Park. She used to come down to see them in her carriage. If anybody was sick in the village she would bring bowls of soup or venison; nobody starved. We used to run up to see her come out of her drive on a Sunday to go to church. It was a lovely sight, the footman at the back, the coachman at the front. The children had to bow and take their caps off.

Alice Farthing (born 1907)

Wash day with the scrubbing board.

Wash Day

Monday was wash day. Mother had a table which was brought in from the bake-house, the bath was put on the top and she did her washing from there. She had a board on which she did the scrubbing down and when the things had been washed they went into the copper to boil. She started as soon as the children had gone to school and were out of the way. She would begin by boiling the water and would do all the whites first. They used soda a lot for softening the water. After the whites had been washed they would be boiled, rinsed and then put out to dry. She would then start on the coloureds. The washing was done in stages from slightly soiled, soiled to dirty. The water that was left over was used to scrub the drain down

and the toilets every Monday. She would also let her neighbour have a bucket to do hers out, you never wasted hot soapy water.

Edna Mills (born 1918)

Hung on the Clothes Line

We never used to have vacuum cleaners, but the floors were always well swept and the mats and rugs would be taken outside and hung on the clothes line and beaten with a carpet beater – that was one of my jobs. You used to beat them hard and the dust would be flying out, probably over next door's washing, but that didn't matter.

Jim Appleby (born 1925)

Salt and Pepper Mash

We never had what you would call big, expensive meals, but the food was always nourishing. Sometimes for breakfast we would have salt and pepper mash. The bread would be soaked in hot water, with a little bit of butter, a bit of seasoning, and it was hot. It served the purpose of warming you up to start the day, or if you could afford it you might have a milk sop.

Les Crick (born 1906)

Stone Picking

My mother was born at Stisted and then moved to Aldham. They used to have to pay a penny a week to go to school. Her mother died when she was forty, very young, and so my grandfather married a second time and

Lilian Crick's mother Laura and father William, c. 1880.

her stepmother wouldn't give her the penny a week to go to school. She [the stepmother] used to say, 'You go into the field and go stone picking,' and she used to have a heavy apron with a bag on and she would pick up the stones in the fields. Then they used to have to put them on one side, along the hedge – the poor little girls, that is what they had to do. She left school when she was twelve and went straight into service until she married.

Lilian Crick (born 1908)

Prayers at Night

When we were very young we had to be in bed by seven, but as we got older that became eight o'clock; you had to be fourteen and left school before you were allowed up to nine. We used to say grace every time before we sat down to a meal. That was something my father was very strict about and we always had prayers at night in what we called the front room. A lot of people never used to use their front room, but we always did and if any of us had learnt a new poem, we'd recite it, if any of us had got a song that we liked, we'd sing it, and they are lovely memories. I also use to love it at Christmas when all the carol singers came round. They'd come to the door, you know, to sing and my father would open the door and he'd say, 'Come on in, we don't want you to sing out there. Come and sing indoors.' And eventually we'd have a room full of carol singers, so then of course they'd have a little supper before they went.

Hilda Strutt (born 1900)

Jim Appleby aged eleven.

Outwork

My mother used to take in outwork from Hollingtons, the large clothing factory, and when I was young I would have to go up with a barrow and collect some suits or jackets that needed finishing off, or some buttons sewed on, and take them home. Mother would do them and then I'd have to take them back again, get the money, and collect some more. I remember going up lots of stairs and they'd be this long counter with a line of girls serving behind. I think we kept them busy, especially on a Saturday.

Jim Appleby (born 1925)

Cage Birds

When we were young we used to keep all sorts of things – pigeons, chickens and cage birds. My father used to keep budgerigars out in the aviary but we kept British birds inside as well. We had goldfinches, linnets, greenfinches and canaries. We used to cross-breed the British birds with the canaries. We kept them as song birds. There used to be an old man in Magdalen Street, opposite the Prince of Wales, who used to catch them and sell them. He used to catch them with big nets: he'd put the food in, and when the birds come he'd pull the string and they'd be caught.

Leslie Knights (born 1911)

Penny in a Stocking

Mother used to have to save up all year for Christmas. There was more meat at Christmas time than there was in the butcher's shop – it was open house, all the family was there. The house was always decorated at Christmas. Mum would buy strips of paper and we would make chains with paste made out of flour. We used to have a tree – no lights or anything like that – and the only presents we got was an apple, an orange, some nuts and a penny in a stocking. Mum would be up about three or four on Christmas morning making jam tarts and sausage rolls and we would come down and ask whether Father Christmas had been. The day was spent mostly eating and drinking and singing songs. Mum would buy a 'four and a half' of beer and a good time and dancing was had. Boxing day was mother's day – she did nothing. That day you looked after yourself and it was her rest day. You had plenty of leftovers.

Joe Lawrence (born 1903)

Housework

My mother did all the housework herself in those early days in Greenstead Road. I was taught how to help her. My brother was not expected to do anything because boys and men didn't have to in those days. We would have felt most indignant if they'd wanted to, strangely enough. My brother chopped the wood for the fires when he was old enough and brought in the coal. I was taught the rudiments of general housework – polishing, dusting, washing, sewing, ironing and all the rest of it. Mother was a very good seamstress, but I hated sewing and gave it up as soon as I could. She made all my clothes and my brother's things. I was always a large child. I put on weight when I was about eight and I was big and awkward, and she made me dresses, underclothes, everything.

Molly Schuessele (born 1914)

A Buckshee Dinner

Every time when the corn year came round the rabbits would be running in the fields, and we'd all go, all the boys from the schools, and catch them. And Mr Sergeant, who in them days was the head man on the farm, he would put them all in a heap and when the corn was cut he'd say, 'One for you, one for you, take that home to your mum.' And that would be a buckshee dinner. We used to run after the rabbits and hit 'em with a stick. In the summer time all the boys from round about would come down and we'd play games in the middle of the road. I remember the corporation used to come round with a horse and cart full of water, and at the back of the cart was a big spray which we used to run and jump on and get wet. The carts were used for laying down the dust on the roads. If there was any horse manure left in the road from the carts it was soon picked up, all the boys used to be after it. On a Saturday morning you'd get your barrow and go down Hythe Station Road, up Hythe Hill, down Brook Street, back down East Street and home along Greenstead Road and perhaps get a barrowload. If my father didn't want it, someone would always give you a penny or two for it, especially Mr Naylor because he'd got an allotment.

Len Munson (born 1906)

Wages Were Very Low

I don't remember us ever having a stocking at Christmas. We didn't have birthday parties and I don't think we ever had anything like bonfires and fireworks on Guy Fawkes night. We had no money for things like that. When a man was in work the wages were very low. We lived in a three-storey house with a big attic and that was 3s a week rent. There was a tap outside with a cement basin and a drain in the middle. Two houses had to share that, but we had our own toilet.

Elsie Seabourne (born 1908)

A Quiet Time

I can't remember us ever celebrating birthdays, we certainly never got any presents. The only presents that we ever got was at Christmas time. We would get different games, you know such as draughts and tiddlywinks or perhaps card games. It was a quiet time; I can't remember us ever having anybody in. We

Joan Reynolds aged twenty-two.

remember we had a fire one year. Dad's younger brother Mervyn used to go in for decorations in a big way and this year in particular he had done it like a cave under the sea. There was streamers all across the ceiling and cotton wool and fairy lights. Well, when he switched them on this cotton wool went up and there was pandemonium for a few minutes – it was dropping on everybody, it was really frightening. Little Ronnie ran to the bottom of the garden and it took ages to get him back in the house. The next time we took him there he said, 'We're not going to play that game again, are we?'

Joan Reynolds (born 1922)

used to play out in the street with our marbles or our hoops. The boys' hoops were made of iron and the girls' hoops were made of wood. They used to reckon that a wooden hoop was no good for a boy because he'd break it. Even the iron ones used to break sometimes and we'd have to take it to the blacksmith's to get it joined up again.

Sidney Murrells (born 1892)

Really Frightening

My mother had nine brothers and sisters who all got married and we used to go to each other's houses all over Christmas. We used to play games and that until one or two o'clock in the morning. We played 'Postman's Knock', 'Come and See the Sultan' and many others. We used to have a singsong but nobody ever got drunk. I

Hold Your Horse, Sir?

The greengrocer would have a horse and cart, and the Co-op used to deliver their groceries in the wooden box in their brown vans, milk as well. Most of the horses were very docile, but I can remember one that ran away, I saw it come round West Street and it couldn't turn the corner with milk cart and over it went – they often used to run away. We used to earn a copper or two by what we used to call 'Holding your Horse Sir', because all these farmers and people who wanted to come into Head Street or High Street to the bank had to come in by horse and cart, or on horseback, but they wanted someone to hold the horse while they went into the bank. That was how these outside porters, as we used to call them, earned their living. I used to tag on to that, anything where there was a copper.

Jack Ashton (born 1902)

In an Old Pram

When we were young several of us girls used to go down the ladder in the river Colne and pull all the old iron out, clean it and then drag it up to Wheeler's scrap yard in an old pram. He would give us a few coppers for it. One day when we were down in the river we had to come up because the tide was coming in, and as we were coming up the ladder a policeman got hold of us and gave us a good hiding. He then said, 'Now you go home and your mothers will give you another one'. We were crying, he gave us a good talking to and said he never wanted to see us in the river again, because one of these days the tide will come up fast and you won't be able to get out. But we never took any notice – we went down again the next day.

Alice Farthing (born 1907)

Straw on the Road

Whenever there was a funeral taking place everybody used to draw their curtains out of respect. They also used to put straw down on the road outside a house where somebody was ill. It was to help deaden the noise from the horse and carts and other traffic, to stop it from disturbing them.

Alice Twyman (born 1906)

Lather Boy

When I was still at school I used to work weekends as a lather boy in a barber's shop. I would go in about twelve o'clock and I would be working until eleven or twelve at night and on Sunday mornings. One Saturday morning when we were very busy

The river Colne where Alice Farthing and friends would play in the mud, searching for old scrap iron.

the police made a raid. All the barbers and fathers were summonsed. I remember it going to court and old Dad saying that one of the barbers said to the magistrates that the boys were in the warm and dry and learning a trade. They just turned round and said that the boys were under age – you had to be thirteen. The barber said 'What about the paper boys? You let them go round at eleven years of age in all the wet weather,' and they said that was nothing to do with it. There were no safety razors in those days, all open cut, and men would have a shave about once a week for a penny and I would be lathering one face while he was shaving the other. If you didn't like him you shoved the soap in his mouth. Men didn't shave much at home in those days. I've known them to come out of the Foundry Arms, have a shave and fall asleep in the chair, half loaded. We'd shave them, wake them up and push them out the door.

Joe Lawrence (born 1903)

A Special Day

Sunday was indeed a special day. It was the only day we had the Sunday suit on and after that it was put away for the rest of the week. We used to come out of church every Sunday evening and at that time of day it was very popular for everyone to go on a Sunday night walk; didn't matter who they were, people always walked on Sunday nights. Some walked along Lexden Road, some round the Park, East Mills and various other places according to what part of town they lived in, they all had their favourite walk. My dad's favourite walk was down Trinity Street, up Abbeygate Street and round through the cavalry barracks.

Jack Ashton (born 1902)

Ten Shillings in the Plate

I remember one Sunday me and my brother was going down the chase, by the church, and there was an orchard there and he went in the orchard and got some plums. Well the farmer caught him but he didn't hit him, he just told him to go home and tell your father that I've caught you in my orchard. And he came down to see my father and he said, 'I caught your boy in my orchard.' And he said, 'Mr Munson, your wife will be going to church on Sunday and she'll have to put 10s in the plate'.

Len Munson (born 1906)

Three Times on a Sunday

Sunday was the Lord's day and a day of rest. It was the Sabbath day and it was kept. The whole family, mother and father and grandparents on both sides, would attend church, sometimes three times on Sundays. We always had a complete outfit of Sunday best clothes, right down to your underwear. We used to say grace before meals, Sundays and weekdays alike, and would often sing a little grace afterwards. We also said prayers before going to bed at night, but not by kneeling by the side of the bed. We said them on our own, before the light went out. It was nice, people have lost that.

Molly Schuessele (born 1914)

Hythe Hill, looking down towards the river, in 1904. Note the tram beginning its slow ascent.

A Free Ride

One of the things that we boys used to get up to when the trams were running was to jump on the back of them and hitch a free ride up Hythe Hill. We would hide round the corner by the Swan Inn and as soon as we heard the tram start up we would just run out and jump on. We used to stand on the big girder that went round the back, or perhaps on the step if the conductor wasn't looking. He would probably be upstairs collecting his fares but if he saw you he would tell you to get off quick – or knock you off.

Len Munson (born 1906)

They Used to Shovel it Up

In Wimpole Road we didn't have a dustbin, we just had a little sheltered place at the back where we used to throw the rubbish and the dustmen used to have to shovel it up. They would put it into a sack and into a horse cart.

Dorothy Lawrence (born 1897)

Butcher's Shop

We lived above our family butcher's shop in the High Street. The house had three bedrooms on the first floor and one for the maid at the top. We had a bathroom with hot and cold water and a toilet downstairs along a passage near the kitchen. The maid used to do all the housework. She would get up in the morning and make a cup of tea for my mother and father, and then get the breakfast ready, although my mother would do most of the cooking. The maid would take her meals in the kitchen while we were all spread out in the

25

Domestic servants at work in 1910.

dining room. Her name was Emily Baker and I believe she still lives over Fordham way. The laundry was sent out to a woman at West Bergholt. Mother used to take it over in her horse and trap. My father kept some horses in his stable which were used mainly for delivery work. He also had a slaughterhouse out back where he used to fatten up a few young bullocks which he would buy from the market, and when they'd got a little bigger he would have them killed and then sell the meat fresh.

Beryl Watts (born 1900)

Hot Water to the Bedrooms

Our house in Inglis Road had three storeys. We had three sitting rooms on the ground floor and a large kitchen and scullery, four bedrooms on the first floor and four bedrooms on the second floor, one of which was used by my father as a dark room to develop photographs. We also had a bathroom and toilet as well as an outside lavatory. My parents employed two maids who both lived in and shared the big room on the top floor. In addition, we had a governess who slept on the first floor, and a gardener who would come about once a week. We used to play badminton in the garden and there was lots of fruit trees and currant bushes as well as vegetables. The housemaids would come down about 6.30 a.m. and would light the kitchen range for the hot water. My mother always had a morning bath. They would then perhaps do the sitting room, take hot water to the bedrooms and probably have their own breakfast about 7.30 a.m. Breakfast would then be cooked and the children would usually have theirs in the nursery. I can't remember where the maids had their breakfast but the governess would have hers with the family. The servants were paid very low wages – about £10 a year – but of course they had all their food and board, and uniforms. They wore a print dress for mornings and a black dress with white apron and white cap in the afternoon.

Elizabeth Compton (born 1902)

CHAPTER 2

Schooldays

Nellie Lissimore shortly after her hundredth birthday.

Balaclava Hat

I can remember one thing – I would have been about nine I think – and we were asked to knit a balaclava hat for the soldiers fighting in the Boer War, and then we had to write a letter to go with it and read it out in class. And I can well remember writing, 'Dear Soldier, please bring me back a piece of Kruger's whiskers.' and when I read it out to the other girls they all laughed of course and I went home crying. When I told my father why I was crying he just said, 'My dear, you needn't worry because that will please the soldier, whoever gets it.'

Nellie Lissimore (born 1889)

This picture was loaned by Bob Gentry and is of his father George wearing his Bluecoat uniform in around 1910.

We Wrote on Slates

I started at the Bluecoat School but went to St John's Green when it was built in 1898. The headmaster was Mr Cheese, who was a bad-tempered old man. I was a good scholar and got on well at school. There was just one subject that I didn't like and that was grammar. We used to write compositions – we didn't have paper, we wrote on slates.

Olive Manning (born 1889)

The Nuns Were Very Strict

I started school when I was three at the Catholic school in Priory Street. You had the nuns there to teach you. We used to go to Barrack Street School once a month for cookery classes. That only came out just before I left school. We cooked dinners, pies and pastries. We were also taught geography, arithmetic and writing. The nuns were very strict, stricter than they are now – they wouldn't think twice about hitting you: you would get a wallop with the cane.

Alice Cook (born 1894)

Bluecoat School

I stayed at St Mary's school until I was six or seven and then I went to the Bluecoat School. My brother Les and sister Vera went to St John's Green but probably my mother and father thought that there would be a uniform going at the Bluecoat, because school clothing had to be bought. The uniform was provided for by a couple of charities and only about forty of the four or five hundred children actually wore it. My brother Charlie and I were selected to wear the uniform by virtue of the fact that we were poor, although you had to be of good character. We had to go to Leaning's clothing factory to be measured for the suit, although the girls from the school used to knit our blue stockings. I remember we used to have to wear a cravat, two bits of linen tied round our necks, a little round hat with a knob on the top and some leathery type trousers – like wash leather.

Jack Ashton (born 1902)

Rap your Knuckles

I was three when I first went to Barrack Street School [later Wilson Marriage]. Some days I liked school and some days I didn't. It all depended on the teacher, some were more pleasant than others. There was a Miss Eve, a Miss Osborne and a Mr Denyer – he got the Victoria Cross I think, and we used to call him 'Quarter to Three Feet'. He used to rap your knuckles with a ruler. Then there was Mr Finch and old 'Sausage Brown', a lovely old teacher. We got the most stick from him but everybody wanted to be in his class because he would take us for football. I was in Standard 7 when I left at thirteen. You were supposed to stay until fourteen but I had taken a special exam to allow me to leave early.

Joe Lawrence (born 1903)

Needlework and Knitting Lessons

I started at St John's School when I was three and then later went to Parson's Heath. We used to have sums and knitting lessons,

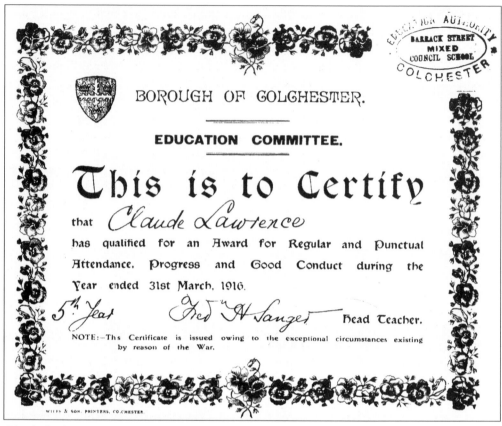

BOROUGH OF COLCHESTER.

EDUCATION COMMITTEE.

This is to Certify

that *Claude Lawrence*

has qualified for an Award for Regular and Punctual Attendance, Progress and Good Conduct during the Year ended 31st March, 1916.

5th Year   *Fred H Sanger*   Head Teacher.

NOTE:—This Certificate is issued owing to the exceptional circumstances existing by reason of the War.

WILES & SON, PRINTERS, CO.CHESTER.

Claude (Joe) Lawrence's school leaving certificate.

arithmetic, spelling and all that sort of thing. I mean they taught you well, you had to learn your tables – I was always good at sums. And spelling, I was always good at that. We went to Barrack Street for cookery and East Ward for laundry. They taught us needlework and how to knit. I used to make my own little dresses when I was about twelve.

Emily Daldry (born 1907)

Couldn't Teach Me Any More

I started at Stockwell Street Infants' when I was five. I stayed there until I was eleven and then transferred to the Bluecoat School in St Helen's Lane. Ten boys and ten girls were allowed to wear the Bluecoat uniform which had to be applied for by their parents and accepted by the charity who provided the uniform. The basis of the uniforms were made by professional people, but the white aprons and half sleeves and little white caps were made by the girls in the needlework class. The boys' white jabots and knitted stockings were also made in the school. We received a very good foundation education. We had arithmetic, a lot of needlework and embroidery. Boys were allowed to leave school after they had reached a certain Standard to the satisfaction of the master at thirteen. Each Standard, as they were called then, had a classroom of its own. There was only the large hall, and perhaps there would be two classes going on at the same time but strangely enough it didn't seem to interfere. I reached the top Standard and for the last three months I did nothing but sewing because the teacher said that they couldn't teach me any more.

Janet Graham (born 1905)

I Enjoyed Poetry

I started at the little Greenstead school when I was about three or four and got on quite well really. There was one class for the older ones and then a big room where the younger ones were taught. There was a low combustion stove in the big room and a clock on the wall. We had desks that three or four could sit in. I enjoyed poetry, I used to sit hours and work poetry out. I didn't mind arithmetic and I loved general work – like history. I really liked all the lessons but I didn't like sewing even though I always got a certificate for it. We went to cookery at Barrack Street for one half-day a week and would have to cook a dinner and then buy it for about 3d or more. There was about thirty in a class and less than a hundred in the school. I got into the top class – Standard 7. I was thirteen when I left school. They had to release me because Mother lost Dad and all she'd got coming in was 5s a week.

Alice Farthing (born 1907)

Paper Round in the Morning

I used to make light of my time at school because I was too much attracted to other

Barrack Street Board School (later renamed Wilson Marriage School).

A classroom photograph from Greenstead Road School in 1914.

things – paper round in the morning, paper round at night, milk rounds, anything like that. On Saturdays, I was occupied with my little wood business. I was so fully occupied in my spare time that when I got to school it was such a contrast with what I'd been doing outside. I can recall a lot of the boys who were at the school at the time, and we were all good mates, but a lot of them are now dead and gone.

Jack Ashton (born 1902)

You Could Leave Early

I started school in 1900 and left in 1907 – that's all the education I had. I went to the West Bergholt school during that period and I left school when I was twelve. In those days, providing that you could pass a certain examination, and you had a job to go to, you could leave early. I remember taking the examination [Labour Certificate] at North Street school and was lucky enough to pass and so that's how I left school. I started work as a milk boy on a local diary farm for 3s 6d a week.

Harry Salmon (born 1895)

A Penny a Week

We used to have to pay a penny a week to go to the Bluecoat School. Every child took that penny on Monday morning. We used to do arithmetic, history, geography, and Friday would be needlework day for the girls. I used to love doing that on Fridays. And one day a week we went to East Ward School – in the morning we'd have laundry and in the afternoon we'd have cookery, that was another day. And we always went out in the playground for drill – you know, marching up and down and doing exercises. We would spend about an hour doing that. And, of course, this was just the girls, we never mixed with the boys in the playground. We couldn't even see them because the wall was so high.

Ethel Matthews (born 1900)

Schoolboys' Strike

I remember the Schoolboys' Strike in 1910. The leader of it was a boy named Kemp, a great big boy. I think he was killed when he was seventeen or eighteen in the 1914-18 war. I remember that they bunged all the keyholes up with horse manure. The boys wanted no caning and an extra half day off

a week. They all got a caning the next day. A fair amount of the children were involved, they just walked around the school hollering and shouting. It only lasted a day. I was too young to join them and in any case I would have got a good hiding when I got home.

Joe Lawrence (born 1903)

Never had any Breakfast

We were so poor, and it's no good saying any different, but we were not rough. I remember at Old Heath school, as plain as can be, they used to give us a mug of cocoa and some bread and plum jam, and I've never forgotten that plum jam – never. The teacher gave us that because we'd never had

Elsie Seabourne aged ninety-one.

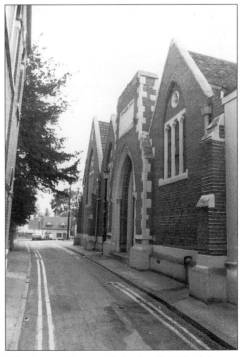

The former Bluecoat School in St Helen's Lane.

Old Heath Board School shortly after its construction in 1894.

any breakfast. Only one more family was like that; we lived at 19 and they lived next door. They didn't pay their rent so the landlord use to block up the chimney so they couldn't have a fire, but as soon as he'd gone the man would get up and unblock it.

Elsie Seabourne (born 1908)

To School on Horseback

The first school I attended was St Mary's in Balkerne Lane. It was a funny little place with just two rooms, a beginners' class and one for the rest of the children. There was a very small playground where the beginners' class used to play, but us older ones used to play in St Mary's churchyard –

never off the path of course, but it was a long pathway. There were about forty or fifty children at the school, some of whom came from the Workhouse across the road. They were brought over by one of the workers there. They all used to come in a bunch and were quite plainly dressed, although they used to mingle well with the other children, and after school they would be fetched and taken back again. When I was twelve I moved on to the Girls' High School which was on North Hill. At this school you had a different teacher for each subject which we didn't get before. Of course, we had to wear a uniform which at that time was blue and silver. In addition to the normal subjects, we were taught French, Science and Latin. We also had a hockey and netball team and there was a school gymnasium. I remember that one family of girls used to come to school in a horse-drawn governess cart – one of the girls would drive the cart herself and they would stable the horse during the day at the Fleece Hotel in Head Street. Another girl in my form used to come to school on horseback and leave her horse at the Fleece during the day. She lived at Fingringhoe and there was no other way she could get in unless she cycled or walked of course. I stayed at the High School for five years and when I left I got a job at a firm of solicitors copying out title deeds, because at that stage I was quite good at handwriting.

Eileen Olyatt (born 1905)

They Were So Strict

I did all my schooling at Old Heath, starting in the infants and then moving up to the big school. The teachers were rather on the strict side, they overdid the punishments. They were so strict – they thrashed it into you. Mr Bates, the headmaster, was a fierce-looking chap and if you gave the teachers any lip they would send you to him. One of the boys in my class was a Dr Barnardo's boy and because he stuttered a lot he was caned because he couldn't speak out. We had a religious class every morning, then history, arithmetic and various other subjects. We didn't do much in the way of sport, although in the later years they started a football team, but as it was such a small school we used to get thrashed by the

Members of Old Heath Community Group outside their club house in Old Heath Road, c. 1920. From left to right: Les Crick, Reg Pettican, Eddie Allen (back), Bob Allen (front), Eddie Amos and Mr Brindley.

Canterbury Road School, c. 1906.

bigger schools like Wilson Marriage and Hamilton Road. At the top of the playground there was a strip of garden where various boys used to look after a small plot each. It had to be done in their own time and there would be a contest for the neatest garden. At playtime we would either play with our marbles or cigarette cards. We used to get the cigarette cards from the soldiers on the Wick. We also had conkers when they were about, and another game involving a key, a nail and some Swan Vesta matches. You would break off the match heads into the hollow part of the key, put the nail in with some string tied on, and then swing it against a brick wall and it would go off like a firework. My mother used to count her matches and would be on to me if there were any missing.

Bob Allen (born 1906)

Nits in Her Hair

I think Canterbury Road school was built about 1900 or 1901, somewhere about the time I was born. It was a big school with three playgrounds. We did all sorts of lessons, arithmetic, writing, history – and I can always remember one teacher that we had there. We used to call him 'Daddy Soar'; his name was Mr Soar. Well he came round the class one day and I was sitting on the edge of the desk, and he tapped me on the top of the head and said, 'What are you sitting like that for?' And I said, ''Cause that girl's got nits in her hair.' Well, if I'd have gone home with them in my hair my mother would have been upset.

Margaret Golby (born 1901)

We Never Saw a Bit of Paper

I started at St John's Green school when I was seven or eight years old, in about 1900. The headmaster was Mr Cheese, who was very strict. When we arrived at school in the morning he used to come round and have a look at you and see if you'd had a wash. He'd pull your collar down to see if you'd washed your neck, look at your shoes and if you were dirty you had to stop in at playtime and have a wash. We were taught reading, writing, arithmetic, all about the stars, England, the Navy and Army and about religion and all that sort of thing. We used to use slates and a slate pencil for writing. We used to have to take a bit of rag in our pocket and we would spit on the slates and then rub it off with the rag. We never saw a bit of paper. I remember coming home one day with a bad report from the teacher and I got a jolly good talking to. My mother said, 'My boy, if you don't blooming well wake your ideas up you'll end up with a broom in your hand.' Well this must have had some affect on me because within a few months I was at the top of the class.

Sidney Murrells (born 1892)

Watching Out for the Teachers

I smoked when I was at school. I remember once finding a big part of a cigar and my old dad caught me smoking it. He told me to carry on which I did and I was ill. But I kept on smoking, five Woodbines were about a penny in those days and we would pool our money to buy some. We would get down the corners of the school playground and watch out for the teachers. When I left school I continued smoking. Everybody smoked then. I stopped smoking before the war but when I got in with the Americans I could buy 200 for 2s 6d so I started again. Wherever you went somebody poked a cigar in your mouth. Then after the war I packed up again and haven't smoked since.

Joe Lawrence (born 1903)

Inkwells With Brass Tops

I started at Great Bromley school when I was five years old and stayed there all the time. The same teacher would take all the lessons in the same classroom which we had to share with another class. I remember that the room had high windows which we couldn't see out of. The desk and seat was combined and we sat two to a desk facing the front. I remember the desks had inkwells with brass tops and I used to get very envious because one or two girls were able to bring a little Brasso to clean their inkwells. In the infants we had slates to write on with a slate pencil and we would rub out the work with a rag or duster. If you had a duster you were really somebody.

Ethel Appleby (born 1901)

Sand Trays

I started at Old Heath school when I was four years old, and in those days they took you right from infancy, through the various Standards, until you left at fourteen. The way of teaching in those days was a little different from what you have today. To start with, to learn your letters you were provided with a sand tray, silver sand, in which to form your letters by using your finger. The teacher would show you how to make the letters and

Les Crick (seated in the front row) with his mother, father and brothers George, Frank, Sid and Bert in 1920. Sid's wife is in the middle of the back row.

Lilian Crick, c. 1921.

to put them together on the blackboard, and that is how you learnt to spell. As we got into the higher classes we were given marks for good behaviour, good work, even cleaning inkwells got marks. At the end of each month the pupil with the highest number of marks was given a prize by the teacher. It might be a book or indeed anything that one asked for in a reasonable way.

Les Crick (born 1906)

We Had To Walk

I started school at St Mary's Infants' on Balkerne Lane, but when I was seven I transferred to North Street School. Mr Harper was our headmaster. That was a bit further away, almost to the station, and we had to walk. We went down Balkerne Hill and along North Station Road. We worked until twelve o'clock and then would walk home for dinner – there were no school dinners in those days – and then get back to school for two. When school finished at half four we would walk home again. If it was snowing, or very wet, we used to go through the Wagon and Horses at the top of North Hill and catch a tram which would stop near enough to the school, and that would cost a penny. It was too expensive to do that every day.

Lilian Crick (born 1908)

Head Lice at School

Our school was over two miles away which was a long walk whatever the weather, although if it was really bad we would stay at home and then the School Inspector would come to see why we wasn't at school. In those days most families were poor and they used to run shoe clubs from the school. You would pay in about a penny a week per child and by the end of the year there would be enough to buy a new pair of shoes or boots. I remember they had great problems with head lice at school, with all the children. It wasn't just the poor people that had fleas, everyone did, even the farmers. My mother used to burn sulphur candles. She would shut the room up for the day and say, 'Don't go upstairs, I've got a sulphur candle alight.' Our parents tried their best to keep us clean; they would wash our hair with soft soap, like a carbolic soap. Some mothers would put paraffin rags through their children's hair, then comb it through. It was everybody's problem.

Ethel Appleby (born 1901)

Prize for Regular Attendance

I started at Greenstead school when I was about four. Every year they used to give out a prize, and every year I used to get a prize for regular attendance, Sunday school and all, just the same. The prize was always a Bible. The teachers were very strict, but it was like everything else: if you behaved yourself you got on alright. I was pretty good at arithmetic, but my writing was not so good and I often had to do it again. We used to have drill in the playground and we also had prayers. Prayers in the morning and prayers at dinnertime. At playtime the boys and girls were separated although we used to talk to the girls through a hole in the boards. The main games that we use to play were marbles and cigarette cards, and then we had another – what you would call a rough game – which we used to call 'Horseback'.

Ethel Appleby with her husband Parker and sons Douglas (left) and Jim in 1937.

One boy would jump up on the back of a friend and try to knock a boy off someone else's back. I always used to be the 'jockey' and would always be the winner. We would also sometimes take our hoops to school and if they got broke we had to take them to the blacksmith's to get them repaired, which cost a penny.

Len Munson (born 1906)

A Posh Dinner

I started school at five and stayed there, at the same school, until I was fourteen. You only went to one school in those days. The school was two or three miles away from Crockleford and we had to walk there and back every day. At one time there was seven of us attending the school at once and mother had to pack up seven dinners. It was bread and dripping and we'd get some water to drink at school. We started school sharp at nine o'clock with prayers in the classroom. There were just two classrooms, one for the little ones and one for those who were older. Several children were taught different things in the same room, one teacher at one end and one at the other. We had scripture lessons, which had to be learnt by heart, writing, copy books where the top line was already done and you had to copy it, arithmetic and history where we learned all about the kings and queens of England. We used to go to East Ward school for cookery lessons, housewifery, and laundry. You used to be able to make something and buy it for your dinner. I remember making a Shepherd's Pie once which I bought for about 2d – I had a posh dinner that day.

Hilda Went (born 1907)

Hilda Went aged eighty-six.

I Didn't Mind Gardening

I remember once when my brother and I were at Old Heath School, they wanted to know about horses, so we had to go over and get one of our horses out and when the boys from the first class came over we had to show them how to harness a horse, explaining what all the different parts were for. And then when they got back to the classroom they had to write an essay about it. I didn't really enjoy any lessons when I was at school, although I didn't mind gardening. Each of the older boys had a small piece of ground to look after and we used to grow various vegetables. There was also a rabbit which I used to

41

Bluecoat School, c. 1910. George Gentry (see page 28) is standing on the right in the back row. Note the cravats worn by several of the boys and the full uniform of the girl in the front row.

take home and look after during the school holidays.

Fred Johnson (born 1902)

Bluecoat Uniform

I attended the Bluecoat School, where my father had been headmaster before being called away to the war, between 1914 and 1919. The children who wore the Bluecoat uniform were not necessarily from the poorer families, but rather they were considered to be 'worthy children': you know, children who wanted to get on, and whose parents wished them to do so. About forty of the children at the school actually wore the Bluecoat uniform which was given out to each child at Whitsun every year. The boys' uniforms and the navy blue part of the girls' dresses were made by Leaning's clothing factory. The girls of the school, in their needlework classes, made part of their uniforms including a white apron, a white tippet, a white mob cap, stockings and then white sleeves to fit into the bodice of the navy blue dress. The boys wore yellow leather breeches, with brass buttons, a long blue coat, a blue hat and little cravats which we, the girls, also had to make during needlework classes. We did this needlework every afternoon for an hour.

Alice Twyman (born 1906)

CHAPTER 3

Working Life

Fred Johnson, c. 1970.

War Work

My first job was at Paxman's and I was on what they called 'Hydrostats', which were fitted onto the mines – this was 1916 and it was all war work. There were crowds working there – women as well – there was probably about fifty working in my department. I used to work on the taps sometimes, you know, putting a thread on these quarter-inch bolts which were then screwed into the adaptor plate on the mine, and for that I was paid about 6s a week to start with. We had to work from Monday to Friday, and then on Saturday until twelve. When we were on nights, we would go in on

East Hill with approaching brewer's dray, c. 1910.

a Friday at six and work until six the next morning, take half an hour break, and then start again until twelve midday. At the end of the war most of us were stood off because they only wanted to keep the tradesmen on.

Fred Johnson (born 1902)

Three and Twopence a Week

I left the Bluecoat School at fourteen and got a job at Crowther's clothing factory in the High Street. My first job was on the 'barring off' machine which was used for making button holes on coats. I earned 3s 2d a week for forty-eight hours' work. All us girls worked in the two big rooms upstairs and below us was the cutting out room. We made suits – the whole thing, trousers,

jackets and waistcoats – or, as we used to call them, vests. You didn't work on everything, you were either a trouser hand, a vest hand or a coat hand. You did the same thing all the time. It was beautiful working there; I enjoyed every minute of it. We had a good boss, a wonderful boss, one of the best. We used to sing to our hearts' content and he never ever grumbled. As long as you done your work that was all that mattered.

Ethel Matthews (born 1900)

All the Way Home

During the 1914-18 war, shortly after I'd left school, I got a job at Nicholl's brewery on East Hill. I started off with having to clean the bottles and soaking all the old labels off.

44

After about two years doing that I went on the horse vans delivering to all the pubs and off-licences. When we used to do the Clacton and Walton run we would kick off between four and five in the morning and have breakfast at the King's Arms in Frating. You could guarantee that the horse would do about four miles an hour. When we got to Clacton, we would go to the railway sidings and there would be a couple of trucks loaded with beer. We would put our empties on the truck and take our orders off and deliver all round Clacton. When we'd finished we would return to the sidings, unload our empties, and pick up a new load for delivery in Walton. We would arrive there between two and three and most likely have dinner there. We would leave to come home about six. You can imagine what the old boy was like: he would have had a drink in nearly every pub, perhaps a dozen in all, and he would sit up there and fall asleep. I would be sitting down below all wrapped up, and when it started getting dark I would get up and shake him awake and remind him to light the lamps. He would then be off to sleep again and the old horses would bring us all the way home. We used to get back about ten o'clock and them we had to put the horses away. It would be after eleven before I got away.

Joe Lawrence (born 1903)

A Toff's House

When I was fourteen I went into what they called 'service' in a toff's house down Lexden Road. His name was Argent. I used to have to sweep outside in the morning and do the step, black-lead the kitchen range and clean the flues. If you didn't clean the flues out right then the oven never got hot. I started work at seven o'clock in the morning and you never answered the bell after ten at night. You didn't have to work continuously all that time but you were more or less always on duty, doing different little things. I had a nice little room which I had to share with two or three others, and I had every Thursday and Sunday afternoon off, but I had to be back by nine o'clock.

Ivy Moss (born 1897)

Alive with Rats

I joined Hyam's clothing factory when I was sixteen and my starting pay was 6s 3d a week. I spent about three months training before going on my own time. I remember that the place was alive with rats and they use to run round the edge of the wall. We just used to shout, 'Put your legs up!' and they used to just go by – we just laughed about it. We saw them about three times a day so we didn't worry about them. They were the happiest days of my life. I cycled from Wivenhoe to Colchester every day for ten years, getting there at 8.30 a.m. and leaving at 5.45 p.m. We used to leave our cycles in an open shed by the road and they were always there when we left off. Nobody pinched our lamps or pumps – they never thought about it. And not once was I stopped on the road in all those years.

Vera Howard (born 1913)

It was Long Hours

After a while I got a job at Parry's Oil Mill down the Hythe. The man who lived next door to us at Moy's Cottages was Dick Ealey who was the foreman there and he got me a job. They wanted someone for 'hooking on the barges' – that was a boy's job. When the barges came in we had to unload the sacks of seed and nuts and load then onto the elevator which took them into the Mill. If we could unload a barge in a day we would get a half-crown bonus. That was so they could change the barge over at night on the tide. It wasn't particularly hard work but it was long hours. Some mornings we would get there at five and not finish until eight, nine or ten o'clock at night. That's when we had the bigger barges up – Parry's own barges. After the seed was unloaded it went up into the holding bins and the men who were working below would then open a slot so that so much would come down onto the canvas. They would then cover the seed with the canvas and then soak it with boiling water. The presses would then slowly come down and crush the seed and the oil would come out the sides. Most of the oil that we got from the cottonseed was used for railway lamps. The oil from the monkey nuts used to go for making margarine. It was all collected in big barrels, some of which probably weighed nearly a ton. We used to push them out onto the Quay and they were loaded onto the barges to be transported to the various factories. The rest of the crushed seed – the cake – came out in big slabs and the farmers used to come for that. Their carts and wagons used to be in and out all day long – it was cattle food.

Fred Johnson (born 1902)

Not Allowed to Lounge Around

I've worked on the land all my life, starting off as cowman and stockman at Slough Farm in Ardleigh. I never had any training as such, I just learnt as I went along. I soon learned how to milk cows – they gave me the hardest one to learn on – that was 'Ginger'. It used to take ten to fifteen minutes to milk a cow. After the milking was done I had the pigs and bullocks to feed – and in the wintertime they'd be about fifty bullocks on the farm – as well as looking after the pony and cleaning out the stable. You weren't allowed to lounge around. We had a horseman to look after the horses and when I got old enough, I became the second horseman. The horseman was very good; his horses were like dogs to him, they would follow him anywhere. You got good money looking after horses but you had to get

Evina Cooper in her ARP uniform in the grounds of St Albright's Hospital in 1941.

there earlier, at six o'clock. You had to clean the horses and see that they were alright; if the tails had to be braided, we would braid the tails up and tie a bit of ribbon on them so they didn't get dirty. Then we had to get the harness right and make sure that all was ready. We had to be out of the stable at seven o'clock. We worked with two or three horses depending on what we were doing, and the big horses weighed about a ton each. They all had their own temperament – some were easier than others – but mine were always alright because I was kind to animals. All animals will treat you as you treat them. If you are kind to them, they will be kind to you.

Arthur Went (born 1903)

Pigs to the Market

I often used to have to take some pigs to the market and in those days we used to drive them along the road. You would start by collecting all the pigs together, from various owners, into one spot and then drive them along in a group. I would go up East Hill and down Maidenburgh Street, along St Peter's Street and Northgate Street and into the market. You never had a job keeping them all together, especially after they'd had their first run, because after that they'd be so out of breath they could hardly blooming well walk. You had to take a cart along to pick up the stragglers.

Len Munson (born 1906)

Pennies on the Eyes

My mother used to go and do what they

Len Munson and his wife Kit in around 1950.

called 'Last Offices'. This was laying people out after they'd died so they would look presentable for their family and relations. I carried on from my mother after I'd been married about five years. First of all you put a big handkerchief round the head to stop the jaw from dropping, then you put pennies on the eyes so they didn't open. After that you washed them all over and plugged them everywhere with cotton wool because after the body has stopped functioning, everything comes out. Finally, you would put a sheet round them before the undertaker came and took them away. You always had to leave the body for an hour after death before you started to allow time

47

Harry Salmon (right), who went on to become an inspector with the Colchester Borough Police. He is pictured with his brother who at the time was a sergeant with the Wiltshire constabulary.

for the spirit to go – that's what we were taught. I can remember my mother doing one just along the road and she'd had a job on her hands because the man who died had been so bent up with rheumatism that she'd had trouble trying to straighten him. Apparently, every time she pulled one leg down the other one went up. She had to go and get a neighbour and get him to sit on one leg while she got the other one down. This had to be done because after death the body gradually begins to lose heat and will start to stiffen. Once you had the legs straight and tied together round the knees, they would keep straight.

Evina Cooper (born 1910)

Job on the Trams

Just before the First World War started I got a job on the trams. I went for an interview and managed to get a start as a conductor and began by learning all the different routes. The rules were very strict: you dare not miss a passenger if he was up the road somewhere. Eventually, I was asked if I would like to train as a driver and I jumped at the chance. I spent some time under instruction on the roads under the supervision of a motorman – that's what they used to call the drivers – and then I had to do some further training in the sheds learning about the various workings of the tram, before taking a final exam before the

General Manager. I can remember that he wasn't a very nice man and he asked me about twelve questions. And at the end he asked me a trick question. You see we were always instructed that we must never use our magnetic brake except under certain circumstances. And he said to me, 'You are going along Lexden Road with your tram at two and a half miles an hour and a little child runs across the road in front of your tram. What would you do?' I said, 'Reverse and give the car power, sir.' And he said, 'Haven't you been told not to use your magnetic brake like that?' I said, 'Yes sir, but you told me that I was only travelling at two and a half miles an hour and at that speed the motors wouldn't generate enough electricity to work the brake.' He said, 'Stop: don't say any more. Get out of my office and don't think you know everything.'

Harry Salmon (born 1895)

Boxes were Flying Everywhere

I used to have to drive the bullocks to the market on a Saturday morning. We used to shut all the gates round the farm and let them out so they could have a good run round while we were having breakfast so they could get tamed down, otherwise they would be away with their tails up. I used to have to drive them from Crockleford to Parson's Heath, along Harwich Road, up East Hill, Maidenburgh Street, then St Peter's Street and once I'd got out of there I used to say, 'Thank God I'm here.' I didn't usually have any problems, but I remember on one Saturday one of the bullocks was looking for a gate open or something to go through, and half way along Harwich Road, by the Flying Fox, there was a gate open and through it went. I said to some boys who were standing there, 'Look after these bullocks for me', and I went in after

Middleborough and the cattle carket, c. 1914.

49

it. Well this chap who lived there had all these lovely little palings round his garden and the bullock knocked them all over and trampled all over his garden. He came out and grumbled at me but I said, 'It's no use grumbling at me, you want to keep your gate shut.' That same bullock, when I got to Maidenburgh Street went running into the warehouse of Joslin's ironmongery shop. There was a door open and in it went. I chased after it and it was tossing its head and boxes and stuff were flying everywhere. And when they started to complain I said, 'It's no good grumbling at me, you want to keep your door shut. You know cattle come down here.' The bullock came out of another door and away it went. When I got to the market I said, 'Thank God.'

Arthur Went (born 1903)

Pumping Sand Like the Dickens

The trams that we drove weighed 10 tons each and the most dangerous part of the job was going down North Hill. They were so heavy that you sometimes had difficulty stopping them. As soon as you gained sufficient speed you released your hand-brake and pulled back your magnetic brake. It was the only way you could stop the tram, especially if it was a greasy morning – we would be pumping sand all the time in order to keep a grip on the rails. I can remember going down Hythe Hill one morning, the first tram down, and I very nearly ran right off the rails. I was pumping sand like the dickens and I only just stopped, the rails were so greasy.

Harry Salmon (born 1895)

Shop Walkers

My first job after leaving school was in the Co-op drapery department and I was paid 2s 6d a week. At first I had to do the dusting and things like that; I didn't serve anybody. And, of course, at that time, you had what they call shop walkers who would meet the customers at the door and ask them what they wanted and then take them to the counter, which always had chairs alongside, and then he would call the assistant to come and serve you.

Nellie Lissimore (born 1889)

Making Waistcoats

I started off at 6s 6d a week at Everitts, that's where I was taught and it was the standard wage for the first year. The next year went up to 12s and by the time I'd got to my fifth year, it had gone up to 23s. After that I left and went to the Co-op where I specialized in making waistcoats. We were on piece-work and I would get about 5s for each one made. I would start by felling all the linings in and tacking the pockets. They were mostly hand-made but if some of it was done by machine, like down the pockets and round the neck, I would get only 4s 6d for that because it didn't take me so long. I could make one waistcoat a day and start another for the next day so my wages weren't all that good, perhaps 30s a week. We used to take sandwiches for our dinner and we would take it in turns to make tea. We used to use big 14lb irons to press our work. They were heated on a gas stove with a flame running through and you just slid your iron in to be heated up. We used to use a piece of rag to pick the hot iron up, but if they got overheated we would dip them into a pail of water until we got them down to the heat we wanted. We used to test whether the iron was hot enough by touching it with a wet finger.

Lilian Crick (born 1908)

Grave Digger

After the war I got a job as a gardener at the cemetery, and later moved on to grave digging. I did that job for thirty-three years until I retired and it was hard work. The graves were either six, eight or twelve feet deep and depending on the type of soil it would about half a day to dig. I still know the whereabouts of a grave that I had to dig for a foreign lady who died and who was buried with all her jewels. They were put in a separate little box beneath her coffin. We often used to have to open up an old grave in order to put another one on top. We used to call the bones that we came across drumsticks. And then there were the pauper's graves, those from Severalls and that, people who'd got nobody or any money. Their burials were paid for out of the rates. They would put two together in a six foot hole with no marker on. It was a sad thing to see; when they were buried the Parson would hardly say a couple of words and then he'd be gone. We sometimes used to open up a grave to put a stillborn baby in. They used to send them up wrapped in just brown paper, some used to have a box, and you could just put them in – you didn't need a parson for that.

Charles Herbert (born 1897)

Lilian Crick (née Oakley), c. 1926.

Horses Weighing a Ton

Once you knew your horses the ploughing was easy. They would walk steady in the furrow and the plough would keep in a straight line. It was when you turned round that you might get a problem, but then again if you'd got two good horses, who could turn around in their own space, it was easy. We worked all day from seven in the morning until three o'clock and then we took the horses off to the stable and went home for dinner. After that we would go back and water and feed the horses, clean them and bed them down for the night ready for the next morning. We did that every day. The horses were lovely old things, you could talk to them and they all had their

Jack Ashton is the second from the right in this group of former railway workers.

own names. They were gentle giants, mostly Suffolks – horses weighing a ton.

Len Munson (born 1906)

You've Got a Job for Life

In about 1919, I went for a job on the railway. I had an interview with the District Manager at Ipswich, and I had to take a reference from both my schoolmaster and the local clergyman. I can always remember the superintendent saying to me, 'Now my lad, look after yourself, don't get into any trouble, and you've got a job for life.' And that's how it turned out. I eventually became a driver on what were then the steam engines and was also around to see the coming of the diesel and electric before I retired. However, like everyone else on the

railway, I had to start at the bottom, with a rag in my hand, cleaning the engines. The engines were cleaned with a bucket of boiler waste or cloths and half a bucket of oil and, of course, they had to be moved to get the half turn of the wheels. We could only do one half of the wheels at a time and the engine-man would have to come and move the engine so we could do the other half. On your own you could spend at least an hour underneath one of those engines, cleaning the different parts, and by doing that you got to know all the parts on an engine. The old drivers, who used to run improvement classes which we would attend in our own time, would tell us, 'When you're cleaning an engine, always ask yourself, "What am I cleaning? – the big end, the eccentrics, or whatever".' And we always took a pride in it. It was a dirty job but they were good times because everybody was sociable and the senior men, the drivers, would always be willing to help you.

Jack Ashton (born 1902)

Domestic Service

I left school at twelve and went straight into domestic service. We had to start at six in the morning, lighting the kitchen fire, cleaning the grate, doing the steps, cleaning the brass, cleaning the windows, washing up and helping with the washing. We worked all day. In the afternoon there would be some sewing or ironing to do and then it would be time to get the tea ready. When that was finished, I'd have to clear away and wash up, and then get the bottles ready for the beds and turn the beds down. After that, I'd probably have a few minutes to myself and would perhaps read a book or do some sewing before it would be time to get the supper ready. When that was over it was time for bed. I had my own little bedroom which had a bed, a chair and a wash stand. There was a mat beside the bed, but otherwise it was bare boards.

Ethel Appleby (born 1901)

I Froze to the Mat

I first came to Colchester to box with the Army and that's when I first met Stockwell, who was the Chief Constable, and he asked me if I would be interested in joining the police when I got out of the Army. The next thing I knew, I'd received a letter from him asking me to come down for an interview. About a fortnight later I sat the entrance exams at the High School on North Hill. I

then had to attend a medical with Doctor Fell who took one look at me and said, 'Ugh, they'll be employing nursemaids next!' because at the time I was only twenty and one of the youngest to have ever joined the Borough police. Well anyway, I got in, and part of my duties were taken up with doing point duty at the top of North Hill and at Headgate Corner. We had to do an hour on and an hour off. There were no traffic lights in those days, you just stood in the middle of the road and controlled the traffic. When we had the bad snow in '57, it was so cold that I froze to the mat on which I was standing and I couldn't move. That was the first time that they'd given us anything to stand on.

Tom Bateman (Taffy) (born 1917)

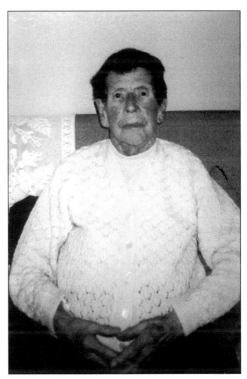

Ethel Appleby aged ninety-eight.

53

A Load of Coppers

When I left school I went straight down the river and got a job on the barges – I didn't even go home and tell my Mum and Dad although they knew I was going. I just jumped on board and by night time we were sailing up by Southend Pier. When we got ashore the next morning the skipper, Bill Eaves, phoned his wife in Morant Road and asked her to go and tell my mother that I was alright. The barge was the *Golden Fleece* and she carried about 120 tons. We used to take wheat to Marriage's Mill, Felixstowe Mill and to Cranfield's at Ipswich. We used to load the wheat at one of the London docks and it took about an hour to load 120 tons. The dockers would do the loading and we had to be ready with our shovels making sure it was all level so that it was under the hatches. I never actually got any wages to start with, but when I woke up every morning there would be a load of coppers there – pennies and all that – and they used to say, 'That's for you'. Come the end of the week I was often better off than the mate who was getting paid!

Bill Warner (born 1909)

11¼d an Hour

In the early thirties there was a lot of unemployment and we used to keep a list with about 400 names on in the Bank Passage office. From that list they used to select about 100 to work on main laying replacements. Those 100 would be kept on for thirteen weeks which would give them enough stamps to go back on the dole. When the thirteen weeks was up they would all be sacked and they took on another lot. I used to have to keep the list up to date, and accurate, to make sure that nobody would slip back. They got paid $11\frac{1}{4}$d an hour which was the going rate at the time. They had to report directly to the job, and when they got there the ganger would give them their tools, usually a fork, shovel and a pick-axe, although they didn't give a pick-axe to everybody because they were not very skilled. When starting a job, they would gather at one end, and the ganger would walk up the trench and measure everything out. And their job was to excavate that bit of trench that day, and it had to be 3ft 6in deep and 18in wide. They were quite strict about that.

Jim Lee (born 1916)

Tom Bateman aged twenty-one.

54

Jim Lee in 1992.

Bill Warner and his bride Hetty Keeble on Boxing Day, 1931.

It Looked Like a Haystack

We used to sail the barge up Salcot Creek, off Mersea, to load hay and straw from the farmer's field. It was just a narrow little creek and there used to be a place up there where you could just turn round and push back a bit to a landing stage that the old farmer had got, and he would come with his old wagons and bring the straw. It was on the sea wall and they'd just walk along, throw the bales on board and we would have to pick them up and stow them away. You had to pack them in a special way – you pressed them between the stack irons, and you'd have to jump on them to get them down nice and tight. When you finished you had ropes that came over and it looked like a haystack. It

was difficult for the skipper to steer because he couldn't see anything in front so the mate would have to get up on top of the stack and shout directions.

Bill Warner (born 1909)

We Used to Sit on an Old Sack

I was made an acting driver when I was about forty. I had a good spell on the steamers and then the diesels came along and we were sent to Ilford on a course to make us diesel drivers. After we'd got used to them electrification came along and we had to go to Ilford again to be made electric drivers. We were open to the atmosphere.

Men and horses from the Colchester Borough Council in the 1920s.

We used to take an old sack with us in the freezing weather and we used to sit on that on the seats, or we would put them up the side to stop some of the draught. You couldn't get out when you were into the tenders and shovelling; you were warm on one side and cold on the other. We used to wear long johns because the draught would come up your legs – some wore cycle clips to stop the draught – that was the most important thing, it would come up through the floor boards.

Jack Ashton (born 1902)

The Horse had Disappeared

When I was younger I used to work on the Co-op oil vans selling door to door around the country villages. We sold a terrific amount of things, although paraffin oil was the main commodity. We sold a whole range of household goods – powders, polishers, lamp glasses, lamp wicks, oil stoves, buckets, baths, kettles, saucepans – anything. It took a while to get used to all the prices. When I started there were five horse vans and one motor van, which I was on. After a while the foreman in charge of the warehouse asked me if I knew anything about horses as one of the other fellows was off sick. Well I said that I'd give it a try and this was my introduction to the horse vans. The horses we used to pull the vans were all cross breeds. The one I liked best was a grey called Bruce – he was a lovely old horse and even when I finished there I used to go in and he would know me. The thing about driving was that you had to drive the horse and you had to sell, and sometimes while you were selling round at the door you would come out and find the horse had completely disappeared. Sometimes it would have just wandered off and pulled into someone's front garden – all kinds of things. I remember on one Saturday afternoon down at Wivenhoe in Alma Street, I had gone down a passageway and I heard the van moving. I didn't take too much notice because very often the horse would move up to the next stop, but what I didn't know, however, was that he had moved into someone's front garden knocking down their brick wall as he went in. When I got there he was just standing there pulling their chrysanthemums up by the roots.

Sid Bland (born 1920)

They were Scrappers

There wasn't a lot of jobs for the likes of us in those days. You had to go into a factory or get a job in a shop behind the counter. I got a job at Hollington's clothing factory through friends. I was interviewed by Mr Walkden, the boss, who was ever so strict. I got the job because my cousins already worked there and they were 'scrappers', and I suppose he thought I'd be the same. To start with you were taught by an experienced person. You had to learn how to do the seams, and you had to behave yourself. After about a month you were put on your own time. I was put in the trouser

One of the best boxers in the old Borough police force was Arthur (Jock) Porter, who is seen here training, watched by constables Tom Bateman, Johnny Edwards and Bill Geddes. Jock Porter was the European Police Heavyweight Champion in 1937/38.

room and you did everything except the pressing and the finishing off. You earned what you did. It was so much a dozen trousers but you never earned more than about £2, and for that you had to work hard. We had to be there at 7.50 a.m. We didn't have to clock in but a man would stand at the door and sometimes shut it right in your face if you were late. You then had to wait until the office staff arrived at nine o'clock and see if they would let you in. If not you would have to wait until after dinner.

Emily Daldry (born 1907)

I Fight all the New Ones

I remember my first time on nights, by myself. I went down the North, and in those days, back in '38, there was the North Gang down there and they were some rough boys too. They were turning out of the Castle pub this Saturday night, and I was going by and I stopped to tell them to mind their language because they were shouting and swearing and there were ladies about. And then a voice piped up and said, 'You're new, aren't you? Well I fight all the new ones.' Well he just takes his hat and coat off and says, 'I'm going to fight you.' Well, I thought, if I walk away in front of this lot, I've had it. I may as well get out of the police. So I thought, 'All right mate, I'll take a chance.' And he said, 'Do you know who I am?' I said, 'No, I've got no idea who you are.' And he said, 'I'm Spud Murphy.' Well I'd heard about Spud Murphy from the boys at the station, and I thought to myself, 'Tommy, you're in for something now.' So I said, 'Wait a minute, then', and I took my belt and lamp off and he came charging into me and I belted him a few, like. In he kept

coming so I let him have it, and down he went. And he looked up at me and said, 'Alright, I've had enough.' So he put his hat and coat on and walked out to the edge of the road and he said, 'Alright, up the hill now I suppose.' I said, 'No mate, I don't know who you are or where you come from, but what I'm telling you is this – you'd better bloody well go there, because the next time you have a go at me you'll get a real hammering and you will go inside.' And off he went. So I turned round, being brave like to these others, and said, 'Does anyone else want to have a go while I haven't got my belt on?' And they said, 'No, we haven't got a quarrel with you.' And I thought, 'Thank God for that!'

Tom Bateman (born 1917)

Nobody Would Speak To Me

I started on the Water Board on the Monday morning and nobody would speak to me, apart from the foreman that is. His name was George Rheumer and he used to travel round the sites on a little motor bike. There were eight of us that started and the other men were all about sixty. We got our tools from a little old shed but they were all short and worn, so I went down to the main works and got a brand new fork, shovel and pick and we went down to Smithies Avenue at the bottom of East Hill. It was a market garden then and our job was to lay a water main in there from East Hill ready for them to start building. The foreman marked out the lengths on the road. You had three pick shafts (9ft) each to get out, 2ft 6in wide. That was your bit, then you shifted forward. I got mine out – my pick was doing the job. The ones that the others were using were like toffee hammers. I got my second one out and they were still on their first, and I was only working comfortably.

Bill Warner (born 1909)

A Coat Every Twenty Minutes

When I left the Rowhedge factory I went to the Colchester branch to see if they would let me do some outwork. I had to see a Mr Orrin and I remember him looking at me and saying, 'I don't think you've left school yet', because I was very small. And he said, 'Do you think you could do it?', and I told him that I was sure I could. Well they gave me six coats to get on with and by the next day I'd finished them. I can still see his face when I took them in and he went through then with a fine tooth comb and said, 'I didn't expect them back today – if you work like this you will never be out of a job.' He then gave me thirty more to bring home. I was paid a shilling each and could easily do about thirty-six in a week. I used to have to provide my own needles, scissors, pins and cotton which was sixpence for a spool of 1,000 yards. I got so used to doing them that eventually I could make a coat every twenty minutes and was earning about £6 a week, which was quite good money as the craftsmen at the shipyard were only getting £3 10s a week.

Alice Cork (born 1911)

Agnes Cork and her husband Albert in 1993.

Tom Bateman aged eighty-three.

Priming it out of the Chimney

The steam was taken from the topmost part of the boiler, the dome. The dome is only an ornament and underneath is a big steam chest cover with about twenty bolts. They take them off to get to the regulator valve. When you opened the regulator that's coming right through from the footplate to there, that opens the valve to release the steam from the highest point to the steam chest and then the valve operates from the steam chest to work the pistons into the cylinders. After that has done its work it finds its way into the blast pipe, into the smoke box and into the atmosphere and if you got too much you would pull a lever and open the cylinder cocks to let the excessive steam out, otherwise we'd prime it out of the chimney. We worked on the little goods engines at 150lb per square inch. Some of

them were 180 but the main passenger engines were round about 200 or 220, they varied.

Jack Ashton (born 1902)

They Fought Like Men

About six or eight weeks later I was down the North again on the beat, and as I was crossing the bridge there were three squaddies (soldiers) approached me. And they said to me, 'It's time you had a bath, isn't it?' So I thought, 'Aye, aye, it's over the bridge.' So I backed up to the side of the bridge so they couldn't get behind me and all of a sudden there was a voice alongside me which said, 'We'll share this one out.' And with that he hit one of these soldiers so hard that he went right across the road and banged into the bridge on the other side of the road. And when I looked round, it was Spud Murphy. He said, 'That's evened it – one each.' Now that fellow there, if it had been one to one he'd have stood back and laughed his head off if he saw me having a good hiding. But in those days, although those boys were hard, and perhaps they'd had a hammering off of us, it was one to one. There was none of this three, four or five onto one. They used their hands and they fought like men, and when you were good enough to beat them they acknowledged it.

Tom Bateman (born 1917)

Everybody Ran Away

I remember one weekend we were digging a trench in Culver Street to lay a new 10in

Bill Warner (fourth from the left) is seen with work colleagues at his retirement party in 1974.

main which was going in between Headgate Corner and East Hill. There wasn't much room in Culver Street at that time; what with Mumford's factory on one side, it was a very narrow road. When you got the trench open you couldn't get down, and with all the other pipes in there we were having trouble getting our pipe through. There was a 4in pipe in the way which we thought was water and the foreman said to break it out of the way. Well it was hit with a 14lb hammer and it flew afire, it was a gas main! Everybody ran away. We filled the trench in and there was blue flames coming up. By this time the foreman had gone and the Council had to pay for the repairs. The gas people came

and went further up the road and drilled their pipe and put a bag inside, and out went the flames. Many a time we would hit a gas service, and the gas and electric people would hit ours. They used to pay and we used to pay, there was no animosity.

Bill Warner (born 1909)

People Pawned Anything

I started working in Priory Street just after the Second World War – there were just two other pawnbrokers in the town at the time. People used to pawn almost anything

Hugh Markham and his wife Nina in their Priory Street shop in 1991.

and we would keep it for up to twelve months. If it wasn't collected by that time we would auction it off. It was a weekly trade and we would charge 6d for the ticket and 6d a month for each pound. We relied on a certain number of customers each week which at the most would be about 200. Some people would pawn their clothing and they would get about a pound for a three-piece suit; if it was a bit rough 15 bob, and if very rough 10 bob. Women made up the bulk of our trade and some of them used to do washing for other people. They would get the job done by mid-day on a Monday and then leave it with us until mid-day on the Friday before delivering it back to the owners. We knew it wasn't their laundry because it was far too good a quality, but it was all beautifully wrapped and it allowed them to have a little bit of money in between. The most unusual thing that we used to have left with us was a horse and cart. It belonged to a man called Wicks and the horse would be fed down on Barber's meadow and the cart stored in Paull's garage. We used to have a slogan that went – 'Borrow or Spend, Markham's Your Friend'.

Hugh Markham (born 1912)

Off the Dole

In the 1930s, the local Borough received a grant from the Government to build a new bypass and they took everyone off the dole to help build it, so many at a time. They would work for so many weeks and then go back on the dole for a few months. We had all types of workmen there from landscapers, office workers, all sorts, and everybody got on together because times were very hard. They knew if they didn't do that they wouldn't get any benefit. I used to work driving a road roller going up and down consolidating the hardcore and tarmac before the concrete went down. I'd never driven one before but the foreman taught me all about how it should be done. How to work it up to the crown on one side and then back to the kerb, it was a skilful job.

We used to have some laughs. I remember one time when a new gang started on the section down near the new bathing place. And there was one chap there – he was a gamekeeper or something – and he must have been well up. He had a bowler hat on, collar and tie, check jacket, breeches and black polished boots, and they put him on wheeling these barrow loads of concrete across this culvert, which was about five foot deep, into the bathing place. Well, one of the men decided to saw this thick plank, which you had to walk across, about halfway through underneath where it couldn't be seen. This was at dinner time and when they started back to work this bloke was the first one across. He was coming across with a big barrow full of wet concrete, all slopping about, and as he got half way across down he went, the barrow, the concrete, the lot into

Bypass workers being presented to Lord Ullswater at the completion of the new road.

The new rail bridge in Colne Bank Avenue under construction.

the water. He jumped up and said, 'Help! Help!' and they all just stood there laughing. When they finally got him out they put blankets and everything round him, but we never saw no more of him.

Dick Thorogood (born 1911)

I Learnt the Hard Way

I left school at thirteen and went out to work for half a crown a week – you know, doing housework and that sort of thing. At school we had a cookery class. As I was very good at it the teacher had said, 'You should train to be a cook.' Of course, my mother couldn't afford to send me, so I learnt the hard way. I went to Billy Mumford's as a kitchen maid up at West Bergholt and I

watched everything that the cook did. And then one day she said, 'You can do the vegetables', and then she let me do the soup, and then the strawberries.

Olive Manning (born 1889)

Come on Girl, it's Five O'clock

My sister got me my first job at Well House Farm, West Mersea. There were four children and the man and woman. I had to get up at five in the morning and you never got to bed before midnight – this was domestic service. Every morning at five o'clock he used to knock on my stairs because my room was up in the attic, and he'd say, 'Come on girl, it's five o'clock.' I had to get his tea, then he would sit down

Geoffrey Gunton pictured at the Food Exhibition in the Cups Hotel in the 1950s.

Emmy Went (end of the row) at her work bench at the Rowhedge branch of the Colchester Manufacturing Company in 1915.

and have a bit of food. Then I used to wash the breakfast room out and clean all the dairies down before the milk came in. When I got paid my 16s, I had to come home and give my mother 10s to help her. Then I'd go to town and buy myself some stockings and a few sweets.

Alice Farthing (born 1907)

Roasting Coffee

My first job after leaving school was for a firm which sold imported meat. I started as an office boy but was later promoted and sent on the road. I used to go round on a motorbike collecting orders and money. I remember that I'd never ridden a motorbike before, but the day before I went out they allowed me to practise round a square of houses in Winnock Road. I stayed there for about five years before eventually leaving to join my father who had opened up a grocery shop in Crouch Street. We sold all kinds of groceries and roasted our own coffee – something that we still do to the present day. In fact, we are the only shop still roasting coffee in the area. The coffee beans have to be roasted to just the right temperature, if you leave it too long it would taste too strong, although some people would like it that way. If you were to leave it and forget all about it, it would taste terrible and, besides, sooner or later you would have a fire. I've been doing it for so many years now that I can usually tell at what stage it is at by the noise it makes as it goes round in the roaster, but towards the end I still have to look at it very carefully because if it's done and you leave it for five or six seconds too long it will alter the coffee.

Geoffrey Gunton (born 1914)

Allowed to Talk and Sing

I went straight into the factory when I left school at fourteen. Nearly everybody went there – the Colchester Manufacturing Company in Darkhouse Lane. I started on 3s a week and didn't have any special training apart from the needlework I'd learned at school. We made coats – alpaca coats and officers' tunics. Everyone had separate parts to do and I was pocket hand. They were all cut out and I had to sew them on to the jackets. There was a forewoman in charge who checked all the work, and if she found anything wrong she would give the work back and you had to unpick it. You clocked in and you clocked out, and they were very strict regarding timekeeping, but we were allowed to talk and sing.

Emmy Went (born 1899)

That was the First Bus

When I left school I went to work for Mr Fale who was the local carrier. We used to deliver parcels to and from town and to the clothing factories. Lots of people did tailoring then. We had just the one horse and cart to start with, and the cart was made of wood, like a square box. We later put that on a Ford chassis when we got rid of the horse – that was the first bus in 1919. We would get the wagon ready about nine o'clock. There was a rack on top where we used to carry all manner of things. We used to charge about twopence to take a parcel to town and we would also do shopping for people, especially during the First War, and we had to queue up which took a long time and we'd be late home. We used to go to Sainsbury's in the High Street for groceries, and there was a place down in Stanwell Street where they sold dead horses for cat meat. If we had room, we would take passengers, perhaps two of three, but after a time when the parcel deliveries died out we took more. They would sit round the side on wooden seats – it wasn't very comfortable. On the way to town we would pick up people and parcels along the way. Many of the women in Old Heath used to do laundry for people in town and we would pick it up and

Husband and wife team, Jack and Betty Austin, alongside their Rowhedge bus in 1960.

deliver it to Colchester. When we got to town we would stop at the Plough yard and put the horse in the stable.

Jack Austin (born 1907)

He Was Completely Buried

Sometime after I left Parry's Oil Mill a friend, Ernie Crick, and I got some work digging out sand pits for Mr Berry near Old Heath Laundry. And on one particular day, it was in March and very windy, and Ernie said to me, 'What do you keep looking up there for, Fred?' 'I don't know', I said, 'Those stones don't look too good, they keep

Fred Johnson aged ninety.

rattling down, and I don't like to hear them.' By the time the stones had started at the top and rolled down the sand face there would be about a quarter of a peck come down. It was about quarter to five at night and I happened to be looking up and I said, 'Look out Ernie, look out. I could see the face cracking all the way down and I was able to put my hands up like that and jump up – I was younger than Ernie and he tried to – but he couldn't, and it came down and caught him round his legs. Well, he twisted round and he could see this big lump – and it came down and went right across him. He was completely buried with just a part of his head showing. I got down there and scraped away and got his head clear so he could breathe, and then I ran down to see Mr Berry. He came up with some brandy and a glass, and he phoned for the doctor, and he phoned for the police, and when the doctor came we were still trying to dig him out. The police didn't come until eight o'clock at night. I was still in Berry's house then because they didn't want me to go home. When we got poor old Ernie out they laid him on a truck and took him into the garage and he laid there all night. You see, the doctor had declared him dead. That shook me, I didn't go to work no more for a fortnight.

Fred Johnson (born 1902)

CHAPTER 4

Transport Memories

A brougham horse cab in the High Street, c. 1905. Note the foot rest on the side of the cab and the long whip carried by the cabby.

They had Their Own Carriages

All the ladies up Lexden Road were well off. It was the richest part of the town, and many had their own carriages. They were painted yellow and black and there would usually be one or two footmen standing at the back as they came down the road. If the lady wanted to get off to go into a shop the footman would get down and escort her to the door, open it for her, stand there until she came out, bring her back to the carriage, open and close the door for her, and then get back to his place again.

Sidney Murrells (born 1892)

My Father Drove All the Cabs

My father loved horses, he was brought up with them, and that's why he went into the cavalry – the 20th Hussars. After the First World War he went to work for a man by the name of Siggers who was the main horse cab proprietor in Colchester. Everything was horse-drawn in those days and my father used to drive all the cabs. In the summertime he would take these big open brakes down to Clacton or Walton which would hold about thirty people, or else he would be on funerals and drive what they used to call a shallibeer. Most of the cabs had a small bar across the back and us boys used to jump on the cabs as they went by and hitch a ride. The cabbies, however, used to keep an eye out for this and would look in the shop windows as they were driving along and if they saw our reflection they would flip their whip back over their head to get us off. You see, they used to carry these long whips and sitting high up there at the front they could see our reflection in the shop windows.

Jack Ashton (born 1902)

My Father Would Hire a Cab

When we were going on our annual holiday to the seaside my father would hire a cab from Siggers to take us to the station. The door of the cab was on the side and you would put your foot onto this metal ring and pull yourself up into the cab. Inside the cab, one seat would be back to the cabby and the other facing forward, so that two people would sit facing each other. The luggage would be put up on top with the cabby.

Alice Twyman (born 1906)

Whip in His Hand

When I was a boy there were more horses on the roads than there were bicycles. I can always remember seeing Wilson Marriage in his horse-drawn carriage. His groom was a man named Webb and he used to sit up on the box with a whip in his hand and his top hat on. He would drive Mr Marriage down to the Mill and then bring him home again.

Charles Herbert (born 1897)

They Would Bite and Kick

There were lots of horses and carts around when I was a boy. All the railway had them, the coal merchants, bakers, butchers, brewers – everybody. There used to be horse troughs all over the place. There was one at the bottom of the Hythe, a square one at the bottom of Mersea Road, one down the bottom of Brook Street, one on Lexden Road, all over the town. They were mainly cart horses, mostly friendly although sometimes you would get a vicious one that would bite or kick. I've been pretty near to it myself. I patted one on the rump one day and it lashed out and I got the end of it on my chest, but it didn't hurt too much. I should have spoken to it first, called it by its name, and then patted it and it would have been alright.

Joe Lawrence (born 1903)

Will All the Men Get Out?

When Siggers used to get a booking for one of their brakes, which held about twenty or thirty, there used to be a little seat at the back called the 'brake boy's seat', and his job was to

Horse cabs wait for hire outside the Town Hall in 1902.

help with the brakes going down hills. I used to get the job sometimes and sit in that little seat. When we were going down any steep hill I would have to operate a rod that went down to the brakes because the leverage on his hand brake wasn't quite enough. I used to operate that when the driver shouted that he wanted it. A regular turn-out used to be a trip to Newton Green. There was a pub there by the roadside and they went there for a booze-up and a meal. My father would drive about thirty people there on a brake, with two horses. On the way home, at Sandy Hill just outside Nayland, my day used to call out, 'Will all the men get out', so the men used to get out – them that could! The brakes themselves used to weigh a fair bit and it wouldn't have been fair on the horses.

Jack Ashton (born 1902)

For a Shilling Fare

We had some friends at Walton and every summer I used to go down there for a month's holiday during the school break. My father would take me to the Castle public house, near the war memorial, and put me on to the carrier's cart which belonged to a man named Christmas. He used to carry potatoes, onions and all sorts of things. He would take me to Walton on his cart for a shilling fare. I can't remember whether it was very comfortable or not but I got there alright. Of course, as you may depend, on the way down there he had to make a stop at the Black Boy at Weeley because he got very dry. I didn't get anything of course.

Sidney Murrells (born 1892)

Norfolk's horse-drawn omnibus pictured in Nayland and probably en route to Colchester, c. 1912.

Life-blood of the Countryside

I used to have an aunt who lived at Braintree and mother would put me on the carrier's cart to go and see her. The journey would take two or three hours to cover about twelve miles, stopping off everywhere. The carts were made of wood with just a cover on, similar to what you see on the Wild West films. The carriers would come in from all the country villages and do shopping for people in the town. Very few people in the country would come into town; they would give their order to the carrier who was coming in. They were the life-blood of the countryside.

Jack Ashton (born 1902)

No Cars on the Roads

When I was very young there were no cars at all on the roads and when they did come along they went very slowly at first. A man used to walk in front clearing the way for them. I can also remember seeing the old penny-farthing bicycles going along and I had an aunt who was very up to date with things and she was one of the first women to ride a bicycle. On one occasion when she was out riding and dressed in a very smart pink and white outfit, she lost control of her bicycle whilst going down a steep hill. Coming up the hill in the other direction was a coalman who was leading his horses and as she passed him she flung her arms round his neck to save herself. Fortunately, he was a big strong man so didn't topple over, but it didn't do much for her nice outfit.

Helen Haward (born 1884)

Rough to Ride On

Trams were the cheapest form of transport I've ever known. They'd generate their own electricity in Osborne Street opposite Arthur Street. They were rough to ride on. From Crouch Street to Sussex Road was a straight length of track where they would go quite fast, the drivers used to test them out there. They were open topped and had wooden seats which reversed which ever way you were going. The conductor had to come upstairs to collect the fares. The drivers had no protection, they just stood there working the handles, exposed to all

the weather, no screen or nothing, a tough old job in those days.

Jack Ashton (born 1902)

Only About a Penny

The trams used to go from the Hythe to the top of the town and down to North station. When they came back they would either go to Lexden Showground, where the Fire Service workshop is now, or down as far as the Recreation Ground. They also went to Eastgates, but no further. When they got to the terminus, they couldn't turn round, and the bloke used to get out and pull the arm down off the wire and walk round the tram and put it on the other side. Then he went to the other end of the tram to drive the tram back. The

A tram stops to pick up passengers in Middleborough en route to the Recreation Ground, c. 1910.

first seats were a fixture but with the rest you got hold of the arm and pulled it over so you were sitting in the direction that the tram was going. When I was barging I would ride up Hythe Hill sometimes, it was only about a penny. I could walk to Artillery Street in about five minutes, but it was just for the sake of going on the tram. The tramlines were in the middle of the road so when the tram stopped you had to watch out that nobody was coming up the road. They didn't come into the kerb. In some places the line branched out into two so that the trams could pass each other.

Bill Warner (born 1909)

Slipping on the Rails

When the trams came up North Hill and round the corner into High Street, they sometimes used to slip on the rails in the wet weather and they used to have a boy there, Bill Bright, who used to have to sand the line until they could get a grip and come round to the points at the top of the hill. There used to be a sand bin against the Fire Office and I suppose he must have stood there all day long. When the driver left the top of the High Street he would come down on a single track until he got near the George Hotel where there was a loop line and a box on the side of the road where the driver would lean out and operate a switch. This was connected to another box down in Queen Street which would show a red light warning any approaching tram to stop because he would be coming.

Jack Ashton (born 1902)

Covered with Snow

Mr Mason, the mailman, used to come up to Greenstead every night at nine o'clock with his old horse and cart and he'd be sitting on top of the box. In the winter time you thought he was the 'White Man' because he'd be covered with snow, poor old horse and all.

Charles Herbert (born 1897)

Like a Converted Cab

I remember the horse-drawn mail cart which used to put up at the Essex Arms – you could tell the time by it – it would always be at the Essex Arms by nine o'clock. He'd deliver the mail that he'd collected from places such as Earls Colne to the General Post Office in Head Street and then put his cart or mail van, with the horse, in the Essex Arms stables. His name was Everitt and he used to sit on top of this little wooden box on two wheels. It was like a converted cab, painted red with the coat of arms on and just one horse.

Jack Ashton (born 1902)

A Tram Ride to Get a Bone

My mother was in the habit of going to town on the tram which stopped outside our house, and our dog, Spot, used to go with her. Mother would sit downstairs and Spot would climb onto the upper deck because he was not allowed inside. When the tram got to the Fire Office they would both get off and cross over the road to Oliver and Parker's, the grocer's at the top of North

Winifred Bunting with father Alfred and mother Drusilla in 1905.

North Station Road, looking towards the station with Alfred Bunting's Nursery on the right.

Hill. My mother would go to the counter to give in her weekly grocery order and Spot would go to the bacon counter and sit himself down until the assistant would throw him a nice bacon bone. Spot got so used to doing this that, one day, he decided that he was feeling a bit peckish and that he'd go up town on his own to get a bone. So he waited outside by the stop and when the tram came long he hopped on and went to town and made his way to the grocer's. There he sat and when he'd got his bone he made his way to the tram stop at the top of North Hill and returned home. This came to be quite a journey and whenever he felt like it he would just go by himself into town and get himself a bone.

Winifred Fairhead (born 1898)

CHAPTER 5

Wartime

Charles Herbert, c. 1920.

The Boer War Wounded

My mother put me in a pram, took me down North Hill, and I watched the Boer War wounded come up the hill in hansom cabs. They had big sandy-coloured helmets on and sandy-coloured uniforms. They were all bandaged up – legs in a sling, arms in a sling, tied round the neck, everywhere.

The people were all cheering and waving flags. They were going to the military hospital. After they'd sorted them out up there they would dress them in a blue suit with a white collar and a red tie. That was the hospital uniform so that they would be recognized.

Sidney Murrells (born 1892)

The Horse Saved me

Some time before the First World War I joined the Royal Horse Artillery. A cousin of mine was already in the regiment and one day he came to see me and asked if I'd like to join as well. I said I would, so he spoke to the officer in charge at Woolwich and I got in. And then, of course, the 1914 war started. I was one of the first ones out, at Mons, and ended up going all over the place. It was rough at the start, it wasn't very nice being shot at. We were on our horses – not like the infantry who could hide behind bushes – we were an easy target for them. I had my horse killed from under me, blown to pieces, and it was the horse that saved me. The shell burst under the horse and it took the full impact. What came through the horse imbedded itself into my legs.

William Moss (born 1897)

Never Seen so many Lice

I joined up just the other side of Cullingfords in the High Street one Saturday morning, and by dinner time I was at Worley. I joined the Essex Regiment and then went down to Felixstowe where I did three months' training. After that I went to France and my first battle was at Arras. We went over the top on Easter Monday morning, that's when practically all our Essex Yeomanry got killed. We followed them over and after we'd had a good many days battling there, as luck would have it I came out all right. We came back to the trenches again and then shifted onto the Somme. We battled there and advanced but we got pushed back. We lost the Essex Cycling Battalion there, they were on our left and old Jerry surrounded them. And from there, just as I'd been fighting, I came home on leave with my rifle and everything. When I got home I had to go out in the shed and have a bath, I was absolutely lousy. You'd never seen so many lice in your life.

Charles Herbert (born 1897)

Killed in Action

During the First World War, when I was working at Walnut Tree Farm as a cook, I started courting a nice boy. When he had to join up he said to me, 'If I come back as I am now, I will marry you.' He went away and not a month later he was killed in action. I said to Mrs Wilson, who lived at the farm, 'They have killed my boy: I have to go and work on munitions,' so I went down to the Britannia and worked there. I worked on the big shells, fitting on the copper bands. We worked hard, from six in the morning to six at night for a fortnight, and then from six at night to six in the morning for another fortnight. There were more girls than men working there and most of the men were quite old. When the siren went a red light came on and we all had to go up to our room and sit with a candle. We couldn't get much food during the war, but on Friday nights we would go up Military Road and have a decent fish and chip supper.

Olive Manning (born 1889)

Sackfuls of Horse Chestnuts

I can remember the actual day that the First World War started. My mother and I were staying at Walton and my father was due to

Troops on the march at the bottom of Ipswich Road during the First World War.

come and join us but when war broke out he went straight away and joined the Essex Yeomanry. When we got home I can remember seeing lines of soldiers marching up East Hill, some of whom were fainting by the roadside, and when they got to the top of the hill they all broke ranks and had a drink of water from the tap or fountain in the wall. Another thing I can remember is there being a shortage of oil and we children used to go out and collect sackfuls of horse chestnuts which were used for making margarine.

Alice Twyman (born 1906)

A Penny for Dead Butterflies

One of the things that we did during the war to help protect the crops from the scourge of the butterflies and caterpillars was a scheme, which was organized throughout the town,

where you were paid a penny for a dozen dead butterflies. And, of course, that was all taken up by the children who had their nets out chasing after the butterflies. Well my father had an allotment and although we didn't have a butterfly net, I did manage to get hold of a bird net which was a clap net that consisted of two long handles with a net on the end, and I would go chasing round the cabbages after the butterflies, and they would be flying up and the net would be clapping together and although I ended up catching a few butterflies, I think I must have done more damage to the cabbages than the butterflies.

Les Crick (born 1906)

Some Were Only Old Nags

They used to keep a lot of horses at Middlewick and that was where my father,

Les Crick, c. 1920.

Up to our Knees in Mud

We were up to our knees in mud and water in the trenches. It's a wonder it didn't kill the lot of us. We didn't get any sleep, you couldn't sleep with that lot going on. There was fairy lights going up, and you could see old Jerry patrolling round, and then there were all these shells and whizzbangs going off. They used to bring the rations up to the trenches. They were rough. They used to do the tea in the same Dixie that they did the soup – well it wasn't soup, it was just some old fat meat and dirty water. But anyhow, you were glad to have it. You used to get a tin of corned beef, a tin of McConnachie and a few hard biscuits – that's what you got. If there was a barrage on you couldn't get out the trenches. We used to have to get a lighted candle and go round all the seams of our clothing to kill the lice. I reckon they were sent for a cause, to keep you awake, because you daren't sleep. If you went to sleep old Jerry could come in and take you back.

Charles Herbert (born 1897)

It was just a Mass of Flames

I remember seeing the Zeppelins come over Colchester. We used to stand on the doorstep watching them going towards London. They didn't frighten us – we just used to watch them. They were like the balloons that we had in the last war but much bigger. They were fairly high up but not too high for us to see their markings. I can also remember going up to London to visit my brother who had been sent home from the war wounded – he joined up when he was just fifteen. While I was there I stayed with my aunt and uncle at

being an ex-cavalryman, got a job. They slept in tents because they had to look after the horses night and day. They were all tied together, rows of them, and if one was to panic it could start them all stampeding. They had to exercise them and get then into condition for going to war. Some of them were only old nags that they'd picked up off the road but they were all destined for France and when they were ready they would be taken down to St Botolph's railway station. They had almost as many horse trains leaving there as they did for the troops.

Jack Ashton (born 1902)

Barnet and one night I heard him call out, 'Dorothy come quick', and I saw this Zeppelin coming down. It must have been about 4 o'clock in the morning. It was just a mass of flames and it took a long time to come down. The next day I came home to Colchester but not before I'd managed to get a small piece of the Zeppelin.

Dorothy Lawrence (born 1897)

We Slept Where We Could

I stayed working on the trams until 1916 and what with the war being on, I was called up. I went to Warley where I was issued with all my equipment and then moved on to Felixstowe to do my training before going to France. I remember being up to my neck in mud and you had to sleep where you could. It wasn't very nice at all. There were shells dropping here and shells dropping there, but I somehow managed to get through it all.

Harry Salmon (born 1895)

Like a Great Sausage

During the First World War I went to stay with a school friend at Brentwood. Her family were bakers and she'd asked me to go and stay for a few days. Well one night before going to bed we were sitting by the window chattering like girls do, and all of a sudden this enormous

Harry Salmon celebrates his hundredth birthday with his son Cliff (rear) and grandson.

Charles Herbert and his wife Jessie.

thing, like a great sausage, appeared in the sky. It was floating along towards London and, of course, all the guns started up, and the searchlights were searching the sky, and all of a sudden it must have had a direct hit because it burst into flames and the whole thing was enveloped. It gradually sunk to the ground until there was nothing left of its covering. It looked like a person's ribs, it was just the framework of the whole thing. This, of course, was the time when all these Zeppelins were coming over and I believe that this was one of the first which was brought down.

Winifred Fairhead (born 1898)

We Would Shoot Them

We used to have to go out on night patrols to try and destroy Jerry's pill boxes. They would shell the road as our transport trucks were coming up with the rations. We used to have to go out and try and quieten them down. We would go through the barbed wire carrying about thirteen bombs in a bag and when we got near enough would throw them in the entrance. They'd be nearly finished by the time we got in there, and those that weren't – well you got told not to bring any prisoners. Those that were still alive would be finished off. We would shoot them. It was either them shooting you or you shooting them. I remember one chap who was with me at Arras, his name was M. from Maidenburgh Street, and he shot his finger off so he wouldn't have to go over the top. Others would put a bullet through their foot so they shouldn't have to go. We were quite close to the enemy and could sometimes hear them talking and playing their piccolos. You had to keep your head down. I remember two lads named Miller from Lexden who both got killed because of that.

Charles Herbert (born 1897)

Food Shortages

I was seventeen when the First World War broke out and I can remember quite a lot about it. We lived alongside the barracks and the soldiers were waiting to be sent to France. We used to have soldiers billeted with us; we would take about two at a time. We has lots of fun and would have sing-songs around the piano at night. There was a lot of food shortages and because potatoes weren't rationed we practically lived on them. One thing you couldn't buy was fruit, oranges or bananas, and not much sugar. When the war came to an end there was celebrating on the streets. We were sent home from work when the Armistice came because we knew it was about to happen, we were waiting for it. It was to be at eleven o'clock that morning and when we heard the news we all went home. There were people in the High Street cheering away.

Dorothy Lawrence (born 1897)

The Armistice was Signed

When the First World War started I joined the Voluntary Aid Detachment as a dispenser. I was sent up to Lancaster Barracks with just one day's notice and I stayed there for four years working in the military hospital. I was still there when the Armistice was signed. I remember looking out at the barrack square, where the soldiers usually drilled, and it was very quiet. It seemed very strange and at about eleven o'clock the bells began to ring and the Armistice was signed.

Helen Haward (born 1884)

Dancing and Shouting

At the end of the war, when the Armistice was signed, people were dancing and shouting all over the place. They were walking up and down the High Street singing and dancing. They were putting fireworks and balloons up against the lamp posts and the police never took any notice.

Sidney Murrells (born 1892)

Victory Ball

When the war ended they held a Victory Ball in the Moot Hall. I went to that with my parents and friends and we danced and danced all night. They had a band playing the music and it was on that evening that I met my future husband. I remember him having to ask my mother and father's permission to dance with me.

Beryl Watts (born 1900)

The Mayor, Cllr George Wright, announces the signing of the Armistice form the balcony of the Town Hall, November 1918.

The Streets Were Crowded

On the night of the Armistice I can remember being taken by my mother up to the hospital carrying a big Union Jack and a basket of apples. The streets were crowded with people milling around and I remember feeling a little frightened.

Alice Twyman (born 1906)

Everyone was Scared Stiff

When the Second War started and the sirens went off, everyone was scared stiff, but nothing happened, and it wasn't until 1940 that there was any trouble. We had to black out the windows and we had a Morrison shelter indoors in the living room. It was made of iron and about six foot by four foot with a cage or wire round the side. My husband worked at Paxman's on submarine engines, and although he wasn't called up he still had to do his turn on fire-watching duty. His only problem was that he only had one good eye and couldn't see very well in the dark so I had to take him down to get his helmet and show him where to go. On his way back, if it was still dark, he had to count the trees in the road to find his way home.

Emily Daldry (born 1907)

Blackout

We had to black out very strictly at the time. We had an air-raid warden living opposite, named Bill Scrutton – I'm sure people will remember him – he was a small man but he made himself heard. He would come rattling very hard on your front door and would tell you, in no uncertain terms, to cover up every crack in your windows, because some light was showing. We often got up in the middle of the night and I would go to the bedroom window to see what was going on. One night I saw what looked like the whole of Colchester ablaze and that was when St Botolph's Corner got hit. We could see the glow from Old Heath. I went to see it the next morning. I should have been at school of course, but like many other children I took the morning off. It was absolute chaos down there. There were hose pipes all over the place and water was running everywhere.

John Hedges (born 1931)

We Just Had to Carry On

I had to do my share of fire-watching. One night a week I would report to my post, which was in Wyre Street, and that's where I'd stop until the siren went. Then I'd then put my helmet on and parade up and down the street so that if anything was to fall I'd be in a position to put it out. We had to stay on duty until six in the morning, after which time the Army would take charge of things. When I got home I'd just have time to have some breakfast and then have to go off to work. We just had to carry on.

Len Munson (born 1906)

Air-raid Patrol

During the war I got involved with the ARP and I've still got my whistle. When the siren went I would have to go round blowing a whistle in case some people hadn't heard it. We had to make sure that all the windows were blacked out, that the shutters were up and there was no light showing. When the All Clear went we would take it in turns to go round again blowing the whistle.

Arthur Went (born 1903)

I Remember Feeling Frightened

I can remember standing in the doorway when Chamberlain came on the radio

Arthur Went aged ninety-seven.

Jim Appleby as a choirboy, c. 1938.

Sand-bagging the Town Hall

One of my early memories of the war is helping to sand-bag the front of the town hall. I was about fourteen at the time and can remember reading a notice in the local paper saying that they needed volunteers to help fill sand bags. My cousin and I decided to respond and we went along to the Corporation Depot where to our surprise we were welcomed with open arms, the reason being that we were the only ones who turned up! We jumped on one of these lorries and went down the bypass to a sand pit near Glen Avenue where we filled hundreds of these bags with sand. I remember that the corporation workmen rather enjoyed seeing us slave away, you know smoking their pipes and giving us lots of encouragement. When we'd finished filling the bags we sat proudly on the back of this lorry as we made our way up to the High Street and the town hall. Of course, when we got there we had to hand the sand bags to the workmen who wanted to do the laying because they couldn't stand and watch us do all the work.

Jim Appleby (born 1925)

about eleven o'clock on a Sunday morning and announced that war had been declared on Germany. I remember feeling frightened because previous to that for about two years my husband had been saying that there was going to be war. Some people were saying that it would be over by Christmas, but I'll always remember Doctor Clendon's wife saying, 'Wars once started are not easily finished.' The first air-raid siren went off a few minutes later and my husband and I just looked at each other – there was nothing that we could do, we didn't know what to do. Thankfully, it was a false alarm.

Emily Tricker (born 1906)

We Had to Sleep on the Floor

I was thirteen when war was declared in September 1939 and my mother had died about a fortnight earlier. It didn't mean much to us then, all we were interested in was being evacuated. I was put on a train at Liverpool Street and taken down to Wiltshire where I lived with a Mrs Coxcox who took in eleven evacuees. We had to sleep on the floor in army blankets.

Unfortunately, the blankets were infected and we all came out with scabies, so we were quickly called the 'Filthy Londoners' and after a week I hitched a ride on a milk lorry back to London. My father was disgusted with me and said that he couldn't help me and that I would have to manage the best I could, so I got a job at Sainsbury's in Watney Street, still aged thirteen, and got lodgings with some Jews. You could get away with that during the war because everything was in turmoil and after about a year I moved on and joined the Mobile Land Army where you never spent more than a couple of weeks on any one farm, so there was no way of tracing your age.

Daphne Pushman (born 1926)

Air-raid Shelter

I made my own air-raid shelter in the back garden. I made up the frame of a shed and just kept digging in the ground and dropping the shed down and down until I got to the bottom. I got a little 10s car lamp and kept that alight in there all the time which also helped to keep it warm. I put a couple of boards across to sit on because the woman next door used to come in with her two little kiddies when we had a raid.

Fred Johnson (born 1902)

We would go and Sit in the Ditch

We didn't have a proper air-raid shelter and sometimes we would go and sit in the ditch at the end of the garden rather than be inside. I remember once when we where down there a doodlebug came over, and I said to my wife, 'You'll be alright, the light is still on, it won't come down yet.' We then saw it go out and it came down at Eight Ash Green. Of course, being in the country we were never short of food because we had plenty of things in the garden. We still had to be careful though because we were rationed with meat, sugar and butter.

Arthur Went (born 1903)

Rough Camp Beds to Lie On

I remember the time when my mother, my younger brother and sister and I were

Daphne Pushman and her father Ted in 1940.

87

A group of Essex children being evacuated.

evacuated. I'm not sure why we went, whether it was because of the bombing, or the threat of invasion. We left from Wilson Marriage School and went by bus to North station and were put on a train. I know that we were shunted about during the day but we didn't know where we were going because the names of the stations had been removed. We finally arrived at Stoke-on-Trent and it was dark when we got there. We were all taken to a church and were given these rough camp beds to lie on. I think my mother and our next door neighbour lay down on their coats. The next day they came to billet everyone. It was difficult for us because my mother had got three small children and nobody really wanted that. We were finally sent to a miner's house which was like one of the houses you see in *Coronation Street* – with a passage running down the back. I can remember him coming home from work, very black, with just his eyes showing. We were given money to run along to the corner shop to buy some sweets. It was impossible for us to remain there and I can remember my mother being very agitated and going along to the town hall to complain. She made a bit of a fuss and mentioned that her brother-in-law was the Mayor of Colchester, so we were moved to a semi-detached house in a rather nice area.

Joy Cardy (born 1934)

We Made a Party of it

We hardly ever used the shelter that we had in the garden because we lived opposite Hamilton Road school and they had shelters in the playground which the local residents could use when it was not during school hours. They used to get pretty full, always the same people, we were all neighbours, so we made a party of it. We talked, sang and played cards. There wasn't much light and the only sanitation was a bucket behind a curtain. The children were a bit of trouble because they didn't like being brought out of their beds.

Molly Schuessele (born 1914)

Just Turned up at Someone's Door

We thought being evacuated was a big adventure to be quite honest; whether our mothers shed a little tear as we departed, I wouldn't know. The fact that we didn't know where we were going made it even more exciting. The train left about four o'clock in the afternoon and the first stop was Cambridge where we were allowed a little time to stretch our legs and use the toilet. We then continued with numerable unscheduled stops through the night, eventually arriving at Kettering. This was about midnight and we were given a mug of cocoa and a biscuit. We were then taken to an open-air school in Beatrice Road, and bedded down for the night. In the morning

Derek (left) and Michael Blowers pictured in 1938.

89

John Hedges and his sister Hazel, c. 1937.

the night at the school and slept on camp beds. We had five blankets between us. I shall be writing later on. I must close now, Mr and Mrs Coles are waiting to take us out. Love to Mummy and Daddy, from Michael and Derek.'

Derek Blowers (born 1930)

Arguing on the Doorstep

My eldest sister and I were evacuated some time around 1940. I can remember us walking from Old Heath to North station and getting as far as North Station Road and meeting a very long queue of other children and their mothers. When we got to the station we were given a label to put on our collars and then put on a train. I can't remember in which direction we went but we ended up in Peterborough where we had to spend the night in one of the waiting rooms. The next morning we boarded another train that took us to Kettering. There we met up with hundreds of other children in this big school hall, and we must have spent the day there because it was dark in the evening when we went down to Burton Latimer, a small village about five or six miles away. When we got there we were all sat around in this room, clutching our carrier bags which contained our gas masks and, I suppose, a little lunch that we had brought along. My sister and I weren't chosen at the time so we were taken by the Evacuee Officer to a house in Dark Street where a big argument took place on the doorstep of this lady's house. She made it quite clear that she wasn't going to have any children and they were arguing on the doorstep saying, 'Well, you've got to.' We ended up spending the night there but the

we were assembled into small groups, maybe ten or so in each group, and taken round the streets of Kettering by a billeting officer, knocking on various doors and asking the householder if they would take in one or two evacuees. As far I'm aware, nothing had been pre-arranged, we just turned up at someone's door. My brother and I were eventually taken in by a middle-aged couple who had no children of their own. I don't recall there being any problems, and although we occasionally got up to some mischief, they just laughed it off. I still have a letter that I wrote home to my mother after we had arrived which reads: 'My Dear Mummy, Michael and I are at Kettering staying with Mr and Mrs Coles. We spent next morning we were taken back to the little room in Burton where we were given a banana each. It seems petty now, but bananas were very rare and were something special during the war. Eventually, this elderly couple came along and said that they would take us and we both stayed with them for quite some time.

John Hedges (born 1931)

It was Like a Cattle Market

In September 1940, when I was a young teacher at East Ward School, it was decided that at Colchester the children and as many people as possible should be evacuated there and then. It was thought that if Hitler was going to invade it would be then – the tides were right, the moon was right and there was known to be a lot of activity going on at the other side of the Channel. So a few days later, myself and three other teachers were taken by bus with, I would think, about ninety unaccompanied children and quite a lot of parents and children to North station and put on a train which then trundled all round England and delivered us to Stoke-on-Trent. When we arrived nobody was expecting us, it was late at night and we were taken to a church hall and given something to eat. We were given a lot of blankets and we told all these children to lie on the floor and we covered them with the blankets. The next day, the people of Stoke-on-Trent had got to hear about this sudden evacuation from Colchester, but they weren't prepared for it. They hadn't done any billeting questionnaires or anything, so it was rather like a cattle market, with people swarming into the hall and saying, 'I'll have that one', and so on until all the

children had been placed. The local vicar came in but he wasn't much help.

Joan Dobson (born 1916)

I Knocked Him Out

My first job with the Land Army was at Thorpe-le-Soken and I arrived on a Sunday dinnertime. I'd never seen a live animal – cow or sheep, bull or anything. The first job we had to do was the milking. You had to put your arms round the cow's neck to get the chain tied. You washed the udders, sat on a stool and started milking. After a couple of weeks I moved on to what is now Colchester Zoo which belonged to a Brigadier

Daphne Pushman pictured in 1941 during her Land Army days.

Len Munson and family on a day out in the 1950s.

Underwood where one of my jobs was to tackle a horse called Ruby and ride it. I also had to work with several Italian and German prisoners of war. One particular day when we were pulling sugar beet one of these Italians came forward and put his hand on my breasts. I turned round and punched him and knocked him out and had to go to Colchester court for assaulting a POW. I remember that Lady Bonham-Carter of the Women's Land Army came to court with me and she stood up and said that the result of this could have been an illegitimate child – that was her statement, and afterwards they just cleared the court and I was back at work the next day.

Daphne Pushman (born 1926)

Supporting the Fire Service

During the Second World War, instead of joining the Home Guard, I joined the local section of the Fire Brigade. Our headquarters was in the stable behind the local pub and we had a couple of bunks there so that every night somebody could sleep there and be available to answer the phones. We were there to support the Fire Service in Colchester. Fire-watching was a different thing, civilians did that. We used to engage in weekly training sessions where we would go out somewhere, take our pump which was towed behind a car, set it up, perhaps where there was a pond, or near a hydrant, run the hose out and start squirting water at an imaginary target. We were all kitted out in full fireman's uniform with wartime tin helmets.

Albert Cork (born 1911)

Didn't Half Make a Bloody Row

I used to be in the Home Guard and was put on the rockets on the Abbey Field. We did our training in an old stable which included learning how to respond to numbers and coming to attention. When it started to get dark about eight o'clock we'd go out onto the field and get the rockets ready for firing. We worked in teams of two and my job was to do the firing. I would get my orders from the command post and then relay this to my mate who was on the other side of the rocket, and tell him to load, say breech number 2. After he'd put the rocket on which he would have got from a heap at the back, he would report back to me, 'Rocket 2 safe.' I was the only one who could actually fire the rocket after receiving a further order from the command post. When the order to fire came through, I would pull a plunger to make a full circuit and away it would go. They didn't half make a bloody row too. Sometimes you would fire just two rockets, and at other times it might be ten or more.

Len Munson (born 1906)

102 Essex Regiment Home Guard in front of one the anti-aircraft rocket batteries on the Abbey Field in 1944.

93

Munitions Work

They wouldn't take me in the Women's Land Army because I was under 5ft tall, but I used to do fire-watching at Peake's Clothing Factory where I worked. When the siren went we used to have to go out on top of the factory roof and keep a look out in case any incendiaries fell. I used to quite enjoy doing that. When I was twenty I got a call to say that I had to go on munitions work and was sent down to the Technical College on North Hill for six weeks' training. We were taught how to work capstans and lathes and other machines for cutting holes and making screws. When we finished our training we were packed off to Letchworth where we worked in a factory making component parts for Spitfires and Hurricanes.

Joan Reynolds (born 1922)

Terribly Burned by the Fires

I worked for the Red Cross during the war and we used to do our training down Port Lane. We had to work different shifts and would turn up and wait for the siren. We spent our time practising how to fit bandages and give injections, and listening to various lectures on what we would need to do in an emergency. If there was a raid on and we were called out, we would travel there in our mobile unit which was fitted out like a dispensary. We would stand along the sides of the vehicle hanging on to straps as we went along. I remember one particular incident occurring at Chitts Hill where a train approaching Colchester had been machine-gunned. There was one woman who was coming into Colchester to have

her baby and she was shot in the stomach and died. And there was a man who was a pianist who injured his hands. I can also remember the time when the Dutch liner, the *Simon Bolivar*, went down in the North Sea. I was sent to the Essex County Hospital to help all these poor boys who had been terribly burned by the fires on board – I believe they were the first casualties in the town.

Emily Tricker (born 1906)

Some Mother's Son

One of the first casualties that we had to attend to was a German pilot from a plane that our boys had shot down. When they found the wreckage they had a job to locate his body because the plane had hit the ground so hard, he was buried three feet into the ground. They brought him back to St Albright's and he was dead. We had to wash and clean him in the sluice room. He was then put in a coffin and given a proper funeral service in St Albright's church and buried outside. I remember one of the nurses saying to me, 'Some mother's son.' He was a young man, about twenty.

Evina Cooper (born 1910)

They Were Killed Outright

When the first bomb dropped on the laundry I was standing just a few yards away in the garden. I had been picking up walnuts when I heard the plane come over. I got behind the tree and the bomb hit the boiler house. Three of the girls

Members of the St John Ambulance and Red Cross at St Albright's Hospital, Stanway. Evina Cooper is seated on the left in the front row.

Old Heath Laundry, where three female workers were killed by an air raid while eating their lunch in the mess room in 1940.

Blomfield's furniture store, which was destroyed by fire during the St Botolph's Street bombing in February 1944. The man standing in front of the shop is Fred Parsley.

who worked there were killed. It was terrible, they'd been sitting on the seat where they'd been having their dinner. They were killed outright. They were absolutely burnt, everything had been burnt off them. They looked like bundles of rags that had been burnt and scorched right through. If it had happened just five minutes later we'd have all been back at work and been killed. It ruined the place and the girls were terrified. And my machine, what I'd been working on, was a complete wreck.

Fred Johnson (born 1902)

Both of Your Shops are Going Up

Well on this particular night the siren went off just before midnight. I was in bed on the second floor and my father was in bed on the floor above me. And we heard this thing come along and my father called out to me. 'The front's alight', and I said, 'Yes, and so is the back', and with that we scrambled out of bed and finally went to another shop further up St Botolph's Street, because it was so hot you couldn't bear the heat from the flames. The fruit shop, opposite us, that was burning, Moore and Roberts, the stationers, burnt down and across on the other side of Osborne Street, Blomfield's furniture shop went up. We had three incendiaries on our garages. And then Cheshire's china shop went up, Blomfield's ironmongers and practically everything around that corner. And I can remember Mr Sam Blomfield rang up and he said to me, 'What is happening down there?' and I had to tell him, 'I'm very sorry to say, sir, but both of your shops are going up.' And yet his son John, who was living in Trinity Street, slept through the whole thing. It was so hot that even the paint on the inside of our sitting room was blistering, the windows were all cracked, but thankfully nothing else caught fire. It stopped before it got to Luckings. When we were allowed back in the smell was terrible and everything had to be washed and cleaned. There was ash all over the place. The next day, however, being a chemist shop, my father opened for business and we had to dust every bottle in the shop. I think he was in a state of shock really, he was automatically doing it, and then on the Sunday morning he just collapsed in church.

Edith Moss (born 1905)

The Whole Place was Lit Up

I remember the night they hit St Botolph's Corner. We stood in the street, the sirens had gone and the whole place was lit up. After the All Clear had gone, I went down with my helmet on and my sluice key over my shoulder. It was so hot, you couldn't get very near. The flames were coming out of the windows of the clothing factories and I showed the fire brigade where the hydrants were. And while I was down there the

German planes were coming back from London after bombing and they were still dropping incendiaries. They got one or two into the Britannia Works. The next day it as a terrible sight to see all the windows out and buildings burnt out. The whole area had been hit – Hollingtons, Leanings and all of St Botolph's Corner.

Bill Warner (born 1909)

We Saved the Pub

My squad was on duty when St Botolph's Street got hit in February 1944. The siren went so we turned out and were standing by at the station at Rowhedge. After we'd been there about half an hour the phone

Albert Cork aged nineteen.

St Botolph's Corner the morning after the bombing raid. The Woolpack Inn is on the right; it subsequently had to be demolished.

went and a rather panic-stricken voice said, 'I don't know what you're doing down there but I think you'd better get up here quick.' That's how the call came through. When we arrived at St Botolph's Corner an officer of some sort came up and said, 'Who are you?' We told him and he said, 'Right, you get round the back by St Botolph's station, near to the Fountain [pub] and set up immediately behind that.' This was right in front of the Britannia Works. All around us was ablaze and they told us to squirt our water where we thought it would do some good. So it was decided to squirt it over the Fountain pub to stop the flames getting as far as that, and to cut a long story short – we saved the pub!

Albert Cork (born 1911)

We Saw the Incendiaries Falling

I was on fire-watching duty on the night of the St Botolph's Street bombing and we saw the incendiaries falling. Our job was to keep spraying the water onto the dividing wall between our building and Griffin's furniture warehouse, and to run around and deal with any incendiary bombs. When we found one we would either put it into a sand bucket, or tip the sand bucket on top of it. They were falling all over the place that night.

Molly Hislop (born 1916)

Plucky Schoolboys

My parents used to keep the Singer sewing machine shop on the corner of St Botolph's

Street near the church. When the bombs fell during the raid in 1944 my two youngest brothers, Tony and Derek Leatherdale, went and helped fight the fires with the fire guards. Some of the incendiaries had landed on the roof of St Botolph's church and they climbed to the top of the tower and put the fires out. The next morning Tony, the older of the two, had a bath and went straight to bed, whereas Derek went off to school. He later got pneumonia and was very ill due to getting soaked, hot and excited. Both their names are recorded in the book *Essex at War* where they are described as 'A pair of plucky schoolboys'.

Nina Markham (born 1921)

All Over at the Bang

I was working in the shop when Chapel Street was bombed. We heard a noise and then a terrific bang, at which everybody dived for cover except one lady in the shop who didn't seem to take any notice of it. She just looked round and asked everyone what they were all doing. She said, 'It's a waste of time doing that now; it's all over when you hear the bang.'

Geoffrey Gunton (born 1914)

Dropped in my Street

When the Chapel Street area was hit I was down at the Balkerne outside the dugout we had there. I saw the plane come over North station – it was a Dornier and very low. If he'd hung onto his bombs for another minute he would have hit the barracks. I heard the bombs go off and then the All

Clear went. I saw the meter foreman coming down the hill and he told me not to go home because the bombs had dropped in my street. When I got to the Essex Arms in Essex Street, they wouldn't let me go through. Soldiers were there blocking the way but Mr Collins, the Borough Engineer, saw me and said that he wanted me up at South Street, which was where I lived. There was nothing much that I could do. I had a look indoors. My neighbour came to her door and she was as black as the ace of spades. The soot had come down her chimney and she was shaking like a leaf. In my place, all the ceilings were down. Five houses along the row had received a direct hit, right opposite the New Inn. My wife was

Derek (left) and Tony Leatherdale.

The devastation at Chapel Street in October 1942.

working at the Colchester Manufacturing Company at St John's Green and I was on my way down to see her when I was stopped by the Deputy Borough Engineer who was going through the debris. He asked if I had shut the water off because the bombs had hit the main, but because it was sandy soil the water was draining away and nothing was showing.

Bill Warner (born 1909)

In the Middle of the Road

At the time of the Mason's factory bombing I was working for a firm called Ratcliff's on the Ipswich Road, where Candor Motors is now. I was taking a car for a test run when I heard this aeroplane go over followed by a number of huge bangs. And I remember seeing this big cloud of dirt and dust going up and when I got there I could see that the bomb had dropped right in the middle of the road. I was actually the first one on the scene and there was a lorry on its side and two or three men lying about the road. I went up to the first chap and he'd got a huge gash in his neck and his chest was peppered, and his hand was just hanging on by a piece of skin at the wrist and he was moaning. I'd recently been attending first-aid classes, thank God, and I managed to put a tourniquet on his wrist with a spanner and a handkerchief. Then I remember a policeman turning up and eventually the ambulances. I ran three or four chaps up to the hospital and when we got there I can remember walking into the casualty department and passing by these patients who were waiting to be seen, and overhearing one woman say, 'Oh, they're only workmen!'

Jim Appleby (born 1925)

Heading Straight Towards Me

The doodlebugs started coming over in the autumn of 1943. They were recognizable by their noise, although you could visually identify them by this big flame behind them. When the noise stopped, or the engine cut out, they came straight down to earth. As long as you could hear them you knew you were safe. I remember one coming over towards the end of the war. The siren had sounded about 2 a.m. and we could hear these things in the distance. My wife got up and went downstairs but I decided to stay in bed and lay there looking straight ahead out of the window. I could see this light in the sky in the far distance and thought that it must have been a doodlebug. Strangely enough, however, it didn't seem to be moving and after watching it for a few seconds, I came to the conclusion that it was heading straight towards me. I got up and went downstairs and shortly afterwards we heard this hell of a row as it passed by. I should think that it was no more than 30 seconds later that its engine cut out, followed shortly by the bang.

Albert Cork (born 1911)

Jim Appleby with his new wife Doreen in 1944.

Len Munson aged eighty-two.

Within a Stone's Throw

My mate and I had been doing some hoeing in the field, behind the Royal Oak pub, and we decided to have our elevenses. At the same time the siren went and there was a plane coming over North station and along the railway dropping some bombs. I was standing outside the barn and looking straight down the field with the woods in the front of me, and before I could say 'Jack Robinson' the plane came right over the wood, right over where I was standing and dropped another bomb. I could see that as though it was in my hand. And where it dropped – I often wonder how I lived –

because it dropped just 10 feet or so the other side of the hedge from where I'd been standing eating my bread and cheese. It made a hole in the ground, without any exaggeration, about 30ft across and 10ft deep. But when the bomb went off, I don't know what made me do it, but I went through the hedge and on the top of the crater was a big piece of iron, and when I went to pick it up it was hot. And I often think how close I was to being killed – within a stone's throw you might say.

Len Munson (born 1906)

CHAPTER 6

Leisure and Entertainment

The Vaudeville cinema (later the Empire) in Mersea Road.

The Penny Rush

We used to go to the Vaudeville cinema in Mersea Road which was called the 'Penny Rush'. It cost a penny to get in and a penny for some fruit to eat. What we didn't eat we used to pelt and throw at each other. We used to see rats running about the place and we would shout out and get up to mischief. We used to call the brother and sister who ran the place 'Jesus' because they crept along. One day when we were there I saw a rat and shouted out and I remember him coming up to me and saying, 'If you don't keep your little trap shut you aren't coming in here no more.' On Friday nights they used

An early picture of the new Grand Theatre, which opened on Easter Monday 1905. Within a short while, however, it had changed its name to the Hippodrome.

to have this comedian who would come out on stage and call out the name of something and if you happened to have one on you you'd win a prize. They did to attract customers and he'd say something like, 'Has anybody got a pocket watch or a wrist watch?', because people didn't have a lot of watches then. Well on this particular night he called out, 'Has anybody got a dog licence on them?', and my father had and he won a cutlery set which my sister has still got.

Elsie Seabourne (born 1908)

All Join in With the Chorus

We used to go to the Hippodrome every Saturday evening and we always had to queue. Threepence for a seat in the gallery or, if you took a young lady along, you had to pay sixpence to go in the pits. I remember seeing Jack Johnson, the boxer, and Marie Lloyd, the singer, and whenever they used to sing a song we would all join in with the chorus. We had a lovely time; a penny packet of Woodbines and a ha'penny box of matches, we were set for the week.

Sidney Murrells (born 1892)

Up in the Gods

My mum and dad would often go to the Hippodrome for an evening out. There were two houses in those days, one about 6 p.m. and another at 8.30 p.m. Sometimes dad would take me if my mother didn't want to go. I remember seeing Jack Johnson, the boxer, who used to do a bit of sparring on

stage and Daisy Dormer who used to be a singer. We used to sit on benches up in the gods and would join in with all the songs. We often used to buy a penny-ha'penny pie from Aberdein's pie shop in Wyre Street and take it to the show with us and drop the crusts done onto the people sitting in the stalls.

Joe Lawrence (born 1903)

The Monkey Walk

When we were teenagers we would walk up and down the High Street, the Monkey Walk, which was where boys met girls. We also used to go to the Hippodrome when it was a music hall. We used to pay threepence to get in and there would be different variety shows. I remember seeing Marie Lloyd, Harry Champion and Ramsey Williams. We used to go to the Co-op on Saturday nights and would walk home at midnight – quite safe. They used to have a band playing called the Waldrons. It was ballroom dancing, quadrilles, lancers and military two-steps. A lot of soldiers used to go. This was before the Charleston became popular.

Dorothy Lawrence (born 1897)

A Wonderful Sight

On Sunday mornings we used to go up to the Camp and watch the soldiers parading and coming out of church. There would also be a band playing, perhaps four of five. And sometimes they'd be hundreds of people up there, it was a regular thing. The soldiers would all be in their regimental

Military bands outside the Camp church, c. 1906.

dress, reds, greens and tartans – a wonderful sight.

Joe Lawrence (born 1903)

Aberdein's Pie Shop

We used to go up the High Street, the girls would be there, and we'd congregate for a laugh and a joke. There was a little shop next to Jack's, a sweet shop, which used to sell hot drinks. You could get eight or nine sitting in there and we used to take the girls in there for a drink. Then we'd perhaps go for a stroll and a lark up the High Street. If you wanted supper you went down Eld Lane, near where the Swag Shop is now, to Aberdein's pie shop and there for twopence you could get a beautiful pie. It was very popular and was

open every evening. Nobody would be a nuisance and you could take the girls in.

Bill Warner (born 1909)

Skipping on the Park

We used to have sing-songs at home. My father had bought an old gramophone from the Anchor pub down on the quay and it had a big horn on it. And when 'Moonlight and Roses' first came out my father bought the record, and other old songs like 'Daisy, Daisy'. We also used to play a lot of indoor games likes Snakes and Ladders and Ludo – we had nothing else. At Easter time, on Good Fridays, we used to go skipping on the park. Everyone used to go, boys and girls, it was very popular. Mother used to pack up a little bottle of water and perhaps a bit of bread and jam, and we'd go skipping all day. They used to have these big long ropes which the boys would turn and everyone would join in.

Elsie Seabourne (born 1908)

The October Fair

In October time they used to hold a big fair up on the Fairfield and there would be several marquees and stalls and amusements. There used to be one particular stall which sold fish and a nice lump of bread for twopence. They also used to sell horses up there and when the fair

had finished we used to go up there and take a rope and catch one or two of these ponies, put a halter on them, and have a ride round. We used to have a good bit of sport.

Charles Herbert (born 1897)

It Would Stick to Your Teeth

The sweet shops used to sell all sorts of things, liquorice allsorts, jelly babies, sherbet dabs and stickjaw. The stickjaw used to come in different grades. You could have it so it would stick to your teeth and stop you from talking. It was a toffee and if

Bill Warner in 1999.

Elsie Seabourne with husband William and grandson Philip in 1958.

they didn't put so much sugar in, it was stickjaw. Cater's rock shop was almost alongside the entrance to St Botolph's railway station. He also did baked potatoes and chestnuts which he used to sell in the High Street and outside the Vaudeville theatre in Mersea Road. He always had a trilby on. He made all different sorts of rock and would break it up with a little hammer. You could get a big bag of broken rock for a ha'penny.

Bill Warner (born 1909)

A Very Sexy Play

I can remember when the old theatre in Queen Street burnt down. They used to have these big pictures on the outside wall advertising what plays were coming and the week before the fire I remember seeing that there was a very sexy play on. Later the people said, rather laughingly, that this is what had set the theatre alight. The old door to the gallery is still there in Queen Street outside the bus station.

Nellie Lissimore (born 1889)

No Television or Anything

In those days, of course, people had no television or anything in their home, so they used to go to the Hippodrome or the Theatre. We used to go to the Hippodrome a lot and when people like Harry Lauder came on everybody would join in with the songs that they knew. We used to sit upstairs in what they called the Circle. I remember seeing Marie Lloyd, she was a singer of course, and we all used to join in with the

songs. It used to be a very good evening, we used to look forward to going there once a week.

Winifred Fairhead (born 1898)

Sunday School Outing

I used to go to St Mary's Sunday school and round about August time they used to take us for an outing over to Copford. There used to be a coal merchant in Balkerne Lane named Amos and they used to cart coal about all over the town. But one day a year, the church used to hire his carts, and the men, to take us to Copford. Because they'd been carting coal about all week they had to wash the carts out and as we'd got our best clothes on we had to see that the carts were clean before we got into them. Then they would take us to Copford where we would have our buns, tea and ice-cream. Then we would play games and have races and, of course, have a lecture from the parson about being good and all that sort of thing. When we'd finished the cart would bring us home and we'd get out and sing God Save the King, thank them for taking us out and that would be the end of a perfect day.

Sidney Murrells (born 1892)

Roller Skating

You would meet the girls in the High Street or on Lexden Road on a Sunday evening, the Monkey Walk they used to call it. A policeman would always be on hand to keep you out of the shop doorways, you had to keep on the move. We also used to go roller skating at the Corn Exchange. A lot of people had their own roller skates but you could hire them for a few pence. I've been on my backside many a time and if there was a post there I'd run into it.

Jack Ashton (born 1902)

The Bachelors' Ball

There was one particular dance in the town that was very famous called the 'Bachelors' Ball' and it was held every year in the Moot Hall. There were about half a dozen very eligible bachelors who used to be the patrons of the event and they would invite so many guests each and it was a great occasion. Nearly all the young people of the town used to gather there on that night. Usually a young man would invite a partner

– a girl couldn't go by herself. We used to travel there in a horse cab or, perhaps, get a ride in a motor car. Some of the boys who had a car would fetch you and bring you home. This would have been around the time of the First World War.

Winifred Fairhead (born 1898)

Bathing Machines

Before the First World War we always used to have a few weeks' holiday at Clacton. My father would go to Sigger's in Sir Isaac's Walk and order a horse cab to take us to the station. Those were the days when you only went down to the beach in the morning. You would have a bathing machine to change in. They were on wheels and would be pulled part way

Winifred Fairhead pictured with Patrick Denney in 1990.

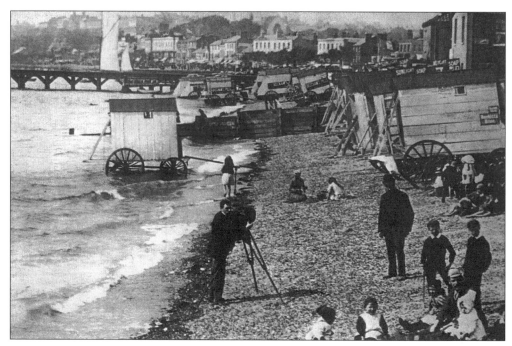

A bathing machine at the water's edge at Southend in the early 1890s.

down the beach to the water's edge by a horse and you would go into the machine by some steps at the back. By the time you had changed into your bathing costume, not a swim suit, and a little mob hat, the water would have come up under the bathing machine and you would get out at the front and down the steps holding onto a rope at the side and plunge about. After that you would go back into the bathing machine where there would be some warm water to wash your face and hands with, get dressed, and then as children we were made to run around a bit to get our circulation going again. After dinner we would have to put on our afternoon dress and go for a walk along the promenade or perhaps go on the pier. After tea, as I got a little older, we would put on another set of clothes and would go off to the theatre.

Alice Twyman (born 1906)

Sunday School Treat

Walton was the place that we used to go for our Sunday school treat. In the morning we would paddle about in the water and in the afternoon assemble for tea. Every Sunday school that went there went to the Parish Room for tea and that wasn't far from the pier. The bathing machines used to be right at the edge of the water on four wheels, like a caravan. As the tide came in they used to pull them up so that they stepped out of the bathing machine on to the edge of the water. They had a horse to pull them down. We never used them, they cost too much and they were really for the ladies. When they finished they had the bathing huts. I learned to swim in the public bathing place in Colchester, which was the open river. They used to put us in a little webbing belt attached to a long pole which the man would hold as he walked along the side of the bank. And that's how you learned to swim.

Jack Ashton (born 1902)

All-in-one Bathing Costume

We used to go to Walton on the Naze for our Sunday school outing. We went by train form North station and would spend most of the time playing on the beach and in the water. Our bathing costumes were all-in-ones with the legs coming down past your knees. You changed in what they used to call a bathing machine which was like a little hut on wheels which would be taken down into the water. The costumes were usually of a knitted fabric and we always wore a hat.

Doris Thimblethorpe (born 1903)

Shot in the Leg

We used to spend quite a lot of our time walking on the Wick and over Donyland Wood. The land belonged to the Army and we weren't supposed to go there when the red flag was flying, but we rarely took any notice. One day when I was about eighteen or nineteen I was over Donyland Wood with my cousin picking chestnuts when, all of a sudden, I felt a thud against the side of my leg. I didn't realize what had happened at first until I put my hand down the back of

A family trip to Walton on the Naze in 1934. The picture was lent by Maureen Cardy, whose father Chris Smith is standing in the back row without a hat. Note the ample clothing worn by most of the group.

Edna Mills aged eighteen.

The Town Crier

The old Town Crier used to come round every December night, round the streets, ringing his bell and shouting out:

Cold December has set in,
Poor man's clothes are getting thin;
The trees are bare, the birds are mute,
A pint and sup would very well suit.

We would usually be in bed when he came round.

Joe Lawrence (born 1903)

my boot and could see blood coming out. It turned out that I'd been shot and it felt just like a heavy stone hitting me. The bullet had gone straight through my Wellington boot and leg and out the other side. We walked out of the wood to the road where I flagged down a passing car and said, 'Would you be kind enough to take me home to Old Heath as I have been shot.' I was then taken to hospital where I had to spend the weekend. They just took one look at it and filled the hole with a white powder. The press got hold of the story and the news placards read, 'Young woman shot in woods in Colchester'. There wasn't any investigation because it was my own fault, I shouldn't have gone through the red flag.

Edna Mills (born 1918)

CHAPTER 7

Special Events

*Helen Haward celebrating her
110th birthday.*

Queen Victoria's Funeral

My father took me to see Queen Victoria's funeral at Windsor and they had a square of eighty-one men, nine pulling down and nine across, pulling the gun carriage with the coffin on up the hill. On top of the coffin was the sceptre and the crown. There were crowds of people there and they had to pull the gun carriage up the hill to where the gate was. I would have been about fifteen or sixteen years old at the time.

Helen Haward (born 1884)

It Stunned the Nation

I can remember the town being decorated and the place being all solemn when Queen

A souvenir handkerchief from Edward VII's Coronation Tea in 1902.

Victoria died. The bells tolled, and then they waited, and then they tolled again. Everybody seemed to be still – it stunned the nation, I think. She was a good queen – there's no doubt about that – she was strict, but she carried out what she believed in.

Sidney Murrells (born 1892)

Coronation Tea

I remember going up to the Recreation Ground for the King Edward VII

Coronation tea. I think it had been raining earlier on so they had to cancel it for another day. I know that the buns and cakes that we were given had turned a bit mouldy. We were given a handkerchief with a picture of the King and Queen on.

Nellie Lissimore (born 1889)

Our Glorious King and Queen

We went up to the Recreation Ground for the King Edward VII Coronation. We were given little bits of chocolate, a bun and a cup of tea. I remember a lady standing in the middle and saying that this little bit of chocolate belongs to our Glorious King and Queen.

Sidney Murrells (born 1892)

Electric Theatre

In my very early days, when I was very young, they celebrated King George V's Coronation. All the schoolchildren, at least all the bigger boys and girls, were entertained on the Recreation Ground where they had a set tea for them and different stalls and amusements. But the younger ones in my age group were taken to the old Electric Theatre where we were given a film show of some sort and when we came out we were given a little Union Jack and a ball.

Les Crick (born 1906)

King George V Coronation Tea

In 1911 we were all marched up to the Recreation Ground for the King George V Coronation and I've still got the silk handkerchief that I was given. There were thousands of children up there and Sir Worthington Evans was the one who presented us with the handkerchief, and also a medal and a little oblong tin box of chocolate with a picture of the King and Queen on.

Charles Herbert (born 1897)

We Sat on Old Wooden Planks

We went up to the Recreation Ground for the Coronation tea on a tram. We sat on old wooden planks built up on bricks and that's where they served the tea. Worthington Evans was in the town at the time and he presented us with a handkerchief but I don't know what became of mine. We were also given a mug and a lot of Colchester people – there were

Thousands of schoolchildren assemble on the Recreation Ground for the Coronation Tea for George V in 1911.

The infant classes from the town celebrating the Coronation outside the Electric Theatre in 1911.

thousands of them issued – a lot of them didn't trouble about them and they got discarded, I suppose.

Jack Ashton (born 1902)

Swooping Aeroplane

I can remember being taken as a child somewhere up beyond North station, towards Mile End, and waiting with my mother and father and brother and hundreds of other people for this aeroplane to come over. And suddenly, out of the air, there came this swooping aeroplane – this would have been about 1911 – and it went round and round trying to find a place to land, I should think. And as it came towards the crowd they all swept off in one direction and then one the other side they did the same. Just who was in the aeroplane I don't know but it must have been pre-arranged and some kind of public event.

Alice Twyman (born 1906)

A Proper Old Rough and Tumble

There used to be two main political parties in the town, one was the Liberal and the other the Conservative. And at election time, one gang of supporters used to congregate down the bottom of the High Street, near Farmer's, and the other gang at the top of North Hill. And then someone would blow a whistle and they would start to march towards each other and fight their way through. I used to be there, I got involved alright, pushing and kicking and shoving each other over, a proper old rough and tumble. They were the good old days, they used to enjoy it and there would have been a few black eyes about, I know that. That was the election. I would have been about fifteen or sixteen at the time. All the roughs of the town, anybody who wanted to join in, could come along and have a fight. There would have been about forty or fifty on each side and the police didn't take any notice providing there was no damage to any property. It would happen every time there was an election. There were two colours, blue for the Conservatives and yellow for the Liberals. Sir Weetman Pearson was the Liberal and Sir Worthington Evans was the Conservative. I used to be on the Liberals' side and used to get a few bangs and kicks. The conservatives used to sing, 'Vote for Evans! Cut me off a yard or two and I'll tell you where to stop; all I want is Evans on the top.' And they'd bring out a strip of blue ribbon, and then someone else would bring out a piece of yellow ribbon. Days gone by – I've seen a bit of life in my time.

Sidney Murrells (born 1892)

We Were Taken by Our Parents

I was at school in 1909 when the Colchester Pageant was on. We didn't go as a body as we did to the Coronation tea, we were taken down there by our parents. I can remember the outlay of the Pageant when they came in with all the shields and spears. It was later revived for the church people and called the Church History Pageant and was held at Lexden. Of course I was older then and my father as one of the 'spares' as they called them. There were a couple or three hundred of these spares, all dressed up in sackcloth.

Jack Ashton (born 1902)

He Would Shout at us Like Mad

I was one of the smallest Rose Girls and was in the front row. I was dressed in the palest of pink frocks and as the rows went back each

costume was just a little deeper in colour until they reached a deep rose with the biggest girls who were at the back. We had ribbon ties that we had to wave and dance to. The Pageant Master was a man named Louis Parker and during rehearsals he used to sit up on a high rostrum with a great big megaphone and he would shout at us like mad. If you dared put a foot wrong, he'd be bound to see it.

Winifred Fairhead (born 1898)

The Triumph of Claudius

I was chosen from our school to play a part in the Pageant in 1909. I can't remember if any of the other children were chosen as well, but I'm sure they must have been as

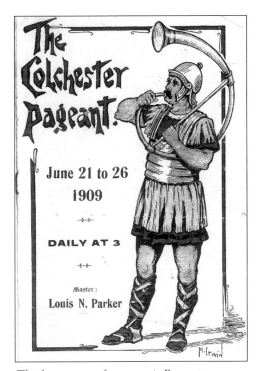

The front cover of a souvenir Pageant programme.

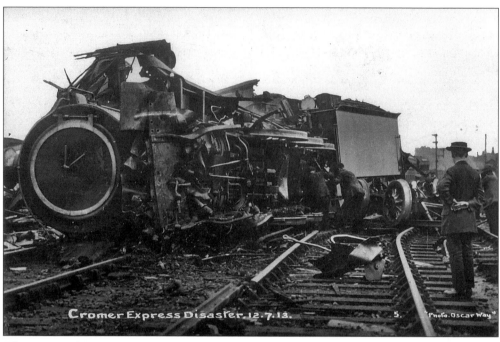

The overturned Cromer Express in July 1913.

we had to attend regular rehearsals. I took part in what was called *The Triumph of Claudius* and I can remember marching in and then standing and forming a guard of honour for someone. There were crowds of people there who mostly sat up on the hill overlooking the arena. It lasted for a week, but on the Wednesday I twisted my ankle so unfortunately couldn't do any more.

Elsie Bonner (born 1898)

Hundreds Came to the Pageant

Hundreds and hundreds came to the Pageant; they came from all over the place. I seem to remember that I went on a Thursday afternoon which was when the residents of Colchester could go at a reduced price. I can remember that whenever the choir had something to sing they came out from under the seats. All the performers were dressed in costume and there were thousands of people there.

Nellie Lissimore (born 1889)

The Cromer Express Crash

When the Cromer Express crashed at North station in 1913 I was about twelve and living in Wellington Street. One of our neighbours, a man named Jim Parker, was a corporal in the St John Ambulance, and as I was walking up the street a telegram boy arrived on a little red bike and asked me where Mr Parker lived. He said that there'd been an accident down at the station. Well, I reckon that I was down there nearly as quick as Jim Parker and as I got to the top of North Hill, near the Wagon and Horses, I passed George Baker, a railway worker, wheeling this stretcher on big wheels which they kept at the station with the driver or the fireman on it who was killed. He was wheeling it from North station – he had pushed that up the hill. I got down to the station and being a youngster they didn't take a lot of notice of me and I went up onto the station. They were stopping people going on the line and all the trains had been stopped. I stood right near to one of the carriages that had toppled over and got a fan out of one of them which I kept for a long while. The engine was on its side and there were loads of people running around but no passengers were killed. On the Sunday morning we went up Bergholt Road and down the field and got against the railway fence and a lot of the debris had been cleared away by then. They'd got two big cranes working there and there were hundreds of people about.

Jack Ashton (born 1902)

Mugs of Tea and Sandwiches

When the Cromer Express crashed at North station, all the trains coming back from Clacton and Walton were piled up at East Gates and on the track at the bottom of our garden. We took mugs of tea and sandwiches down for the passengers on the trains.

Charles Herbert (born 1897)

Les and Lilian Crick celebrate their Golden Wedding in 1984.

Jack Austin aged ninety-three.

Flooded Out

At the time of the bad flooding in 1953 I was working at the Rowhedge Sand and Ballast Company and our small wooden-built office got flooded out. When I went to work the following morning the whole of the main street at Rowhedge was flooded right up to the entrance to our works. Several of the houses around the Anchor pub area were flooded and I remember that we spent a lot of time filling sand bags to help keep the water out. In fact, many of the sand bags were supplied by the Italians who, as part of the flood relief programme, had sent thousands of bags over here. Of course,

down at our place we'd got heaps of sand and there was plenty of people who volunteered to fill the bags which were then sent to areas such as Bath Side at Harwich where they'd had some bad flooding. In Colchester the Hythe was under about two feet of water, particularly the Haven Road area.

Les Crick (born 1906)

A Floating Bed

When my husband and I got married we lived for some time in a couple of rooms in the cellar of the Sun public house in Hythe Station Road. We stayed there until we got flooded out in the high tides of 1953. I woke up in the morning and could hear a knocking noise and wondered where it was coming from. Our bed was afloat and was knocking on the wall. When my husband went to get out of bed he found himself up to his waist in water. Hythe Station Road was like a river. We slept in the bed the next night as we had no where to go. We had a floating bed!

Alice Farthing (born 1907)

It Wasn't That Deep

On the whole the flooding at Colchester was not all that severe because the town is quite high up and the only area really affected was the Hythe. I remember being on duty down there at the time and having to wade through the water, but it wasn't that deep.

Harry Salmon (born 1895)

CHAPTER 8

Reflections

Jack Ashton aged ninety-four.

Conversation is Everything

Most days I go to Eld Lane Community Centre for my dinner. I've made a lot of friends there – people to talk to and get friendly with. Conversation is everything in life when you get to our age. If you don't converse and have a laugh and joke, you might as well not be alive. I have enjoyed reminiscing about the past over the last few weeks very much indeed. It's been a pleasure and interesting for me to be asked questions about the past. Looking back on my life I would say it was the kind of life that one person would find a pleasure, and another might not. Life is what you make it and it had to be because money wasn't plentiful, not to the working classes.

Jack Ashton (born 1902)

Elsie Seabourne pictured with the actor John Mills, during the 1960s.

The Old Days Were Better

I definitely think the old days were better. I was poor compared to what I have now; we were very poor, but respectably poor. We were not rough – we were not allowed to go running about the streets and swearing, anything like that. Even when I got married, when my father was alive, if I said 'damn' he would pull me up. The children in those days all mucked in and played together, but everybody is well off today. Nowadays, I keep myself quite busy. I sometimes go to Paxman's club but I spend most of my time just pottering about, to be truthful. One of the highlights of my life was having my picture taken with the film actor John Mills. He was in Colchester to open the new Cramphorn's shop in St Botolph's Street and as I walked by he called me over and said, 'Would you mind helping me cut this ribbon?', so I went over and stood next to him as we had our picture taken.

Elsie Seabourne (born 1908)

There Wasn't the Crime

In some ways there was more comradeship in the old days. Perhaps I don't see my neighbours for days at a time, but in the old days they would be in and out all the time. They would come in to borrow something or to have a chat and cup of tea. There wasn't the crime in the old days, nothing like it is today. I have been burgled here – didn't have that in my day. If you knew a girl had been out with a soldier you wouldn't have nothing to do with her. You had to be smartly dressed, navy blue suit and black shoes with trilby, otherwise the girls wouldn't look at you. I have a granddaughter aged eighteen and she looks a freak. She has a pair of men's pants, thick tights, a pair of socks and boots and her hair is done in a bun on top. My daughter said it is the fashion.

Joe Lawrence (born 1903)

I Won't Give In

Thinking back, life was better, quieter, it's a racket now. I don't like it. You used to be able to look out and see fields, now it is all houses. We used to walk for miles to Ardleigh and Bromley and never meet anyone. I still look after myself and the home. I put the fire on. I can't keep on the go and have to keep sitting down for a while, and I can't use my hands. I don't have much to eat – I've got a hiatus hernia so I have to be very careful otherwise I wouldn't get any sleep at night. I can't use the vacuum cleaner, it's too heavy. I use a brush and dustpan, sweep round and dust, then sit down and have a cup of tea or coffee. I keep pottering about, there's always something to do, I won't give in.

Alice Farthing (born 1907)

A Perfect Love

My wife and I got married at Wivenhoe church and I've never regretted it. I thank God every day for the happy, lovely times we had together here, for love and happiness. I remember her saying to me one night, 'When we get to heaven, will we still love each other like we do now?' I said, 'No dear, we shall love each other more because it will be a perfect love.' I do miss her now;

Arthur Went and his future wife Ivy Margerum in 1926.

we were together for fifty-five years. Being married is like is like being Siamese twins, you are joined together and when the parting comes it leaves a nasty wound. The wound is beginning to heal but I shall take the scar with me to my grave. That's how it should be.

Arthur Went (born 1903)

You Left the House Open

Looking back, people want so much today, they are never satisfied. They get into trouble. We never had any trouble; I've never heard of so much crime and rape etc. You could leave your house open, you could walk about, take your money in your hand and no-one would say anything. You never had to worry about your purse. When I first married we had a wireless. You made it yourself or had somebody make it for you. There were no washing machines in those days, you did everything by hand. Everybody was in the same boat. You swept the floors and polished them – no vacuum cleaners. I still go to church on a Sunday and to a social club once a fortnight. I knit from morn till night for the Hospice. They bring the wool, new or old, and I make shawls, babies' things, gloves, bed socks, blankets, cushions, tea cosies – I never stop. It's all voluntary, I've never got paid for anything. I have a home help that comes in three times a week and a friend across the road who does some shopping.

Doris Thimblethorpe (born 1903)

Waiting for the Call

When I was young there were no aeroplanes but now they can fly to the moon. The moon was made to be up there and if there's any money to be spent it should be spent here, not trying to get to the moon. When I was eighteen, a missionary came to the village and I was brought to see myself as a sinner – I hadn't realized that before. I gave my heart to the Lord Jesus Christ at the age of eighteen. I've lived quite a healthy life and maybe that is why I am as old as I am, and as well as I am. I think that is missing in young people today, whatever they have they are always wanting something else, no contentment, whatever somebody else has they want the next best thing. Sundays is still a special day for me and now at ninety-three I am waiting for the call. All I know of the hereafter is that God is there and Jesus is there. I don't worry about it, I have my Bible to read and there are many promises in there for us.

Emmy Went (born 1899)

Meeting the Queen Mother

There is no doubt that we have moved on to better times. Things were very hard in the Depression for most people. But although things were bad, nobody complained a lot, everyone seemed to be happy. Nobody had any money but everybody was in the same boat within our circle, and we all got on extremely well. There was no television and transport was difficult, everybody went everywhere by bicycle, nearly everybody did. One of the highlights of my life was meeting the Queen Mother when I was working in East Africa. At the time of her visit I was the Senior Marine Engineer of the East African Railway and Harbours, and she had been travelling in East Africa for about a fortnight before arriving at Kisumu where I was working. My wife, Agnes, and daughter, Estelle, were living with me at the time and when she arrived at the airport we were introduced to her. She said, 'How do you do?' to both of us, and Agnes made her curtsy. Then she turned back to

Emmy Went aged ninety-eight.

The Queen Mother during a visit to Kisumu, East Africa, in 1960. Albert Cork's daughter, Estelle, is standing in the front row on the right.

me and said, 'Oh, yes, you are responsible for the lake services here, aren't you?' I said, 'Yes', and she said, 'It's a very beautiful lake: it is lovely here.' I said, 'Frankly, I think it is more beautiful over on the Entebbe side. You would like it there. The islands reminds me very much of the rocks in Scotland.' She said, 'Yes, I came out with my husband and we stayed over there and had a lovely trip on the lake.' She then turned to one of her ladies in waiting and said, 'We ought to have done something like that this time.' Then she said, 'But then we have done so much. We can't do everything, can we?' And off she went.

Albert Cork (born 1911)

Buckingham Palace

One of the highlights of my life was receiving an invitation to attend a garden party at Buckingham Palace. In fact, I've been rather lucky because I've been twice. The first time was because of my association with the Council of Voluntary Service, and the second occasion was for my work with the Marriage Guidance. On the second occasion, Geoffrey was able to come with me, which was very nice. To enter the garden, you have to make your way, either on foot or by car, through the Palace itself and security is very strict. Once you have gone through you can go where you wish in the garden. The Royal family come out as a group and walk down various aisles.

which are each headed by a Beefeater. I would say that there must have been several thousand people there all mingling about. The catering was done by Lyons and consisted of an assortment of cakes and sandwiches which you helped yourself to. We didn't actually get to speak to any of the Royal family but we did sit next to Edward Heath for a while, who was there with his father, and we had a nice chat. The Queen and the rest of the Royal family had their tea in a separate marquee and I believe that certain people are selected to be introduced to her.

Freda Gunton (born 1917)

I Keep Myself Busy

Looking back on my eighty-four years I would say that times were harder then. Take washing: now we just open the door and shove it in. I don't wish that we had the scrubbing board back again, it was hard work. I enjoy thinking about the past, there was a lot of happiness, people were more friendly. Nowadays I keep myself busy. I belong to the Trefoil Guild, the Women's Institute, the church choir, bowls and the Friendship Club. When I'm not out at the clubs I am doing housework. I was up this morning at five o'clock doing the kitchen out. I made a cup of tea at six o'clock and then went back to bed again until 7.30 a.m. Then I got up again and hoovered round here and did some polishing. I do a bit of reading and crocheting and then there's my garden. I do my brass – that takes nearly two hours – and then there is the cutlery.

Evina Cooper (born 1910)

I Do Everything Myself

Life would be better if my wife was still with me; she died two years ago, and went sudden. Now I do everything myself, cooking, housework and the garden. I had a good wife and thanks to her I am the position I am financially. She never squandered money.

Bob Allen (born 1906)

A Strong Heart

When I was a hundred years old a lovely cake came in the morning from my granddaughter. And there was champagne there and they all clapped. The Mayor and Mayoress gave me a

Evina Cooper aged eighty-nine.

Edna Mills aged seventy-five.

red carnation. I said that I would like to thank my family and the wardens, past and present, for their kindness to me and for the lovely day. I recommend hard work to live to a hundred years, plenty of worries and a strong heart.

Olive Manning (born 1889)

Life is So Much Easier

Looking back, the way of life nowadays is so much easier – you haven't got to light a fire before you get a cup of tea. I've got central heating here and a washing machine. On the down side, the children today haven't got the freedom and the pleasures that we had. They haven't got the 'Penny Rush' like we had at the Empire. Children all sit in front of the television now, and that isn't

good. We used to play games over the Wick but parents today are too frightened to let their children out.

Edna Mills (born 1918)

It's Been a Treat

It's been a pleasure talking to you. You know, it does you good to recall old times and it revives your memory – it revives life. I've really enjoyed it and I feel that I owe you a great big thank you for coming to me because it's made me live lots of my life over again. I always think that I've been a lucky girl, I've had a lovely life and it was a treat to be able to talk to somebody about it.

Hilda Strutt (born 1900)